JOURNEYS

Benchmark and Unit Tests

Grade 2

HOUGHTON MIFFLIN HARCOURT
School Publishers

Contents

Contents

Name _____ Date _____

Reading

Read the selection. Then read each question that follows it.
Decide which is the best answer to each question.
Mark the space for the answer you have chosen.

Autumn Treasures

by Edna Ledgard
art by Helen Cogancherry

1 Grace found a pretty red leaf. She found a big orange leaf and three yellow leaves. She even found a green leaf. She tucked them into her pocket and ran to school.

2 Her friends had leaves, too. Red leaves. Yellow leaves. Orange leaves. Some children had brought acorns and horse chestnuts, too.

3 "I'm going to keep my leaves forever," Grace told Miss Hill.

4   Miss Hill smiled. She passed out cans of old peeled crayons and sheets of white paper. Grace put a leaf on her desk, bumpy side up under the paper. Carefully she rubbed the side of her red crayon against the paper. It made a leaf pattern.

5   Soon Grace had a red leaf, an orange leaf, and three yellow leaves on her paper.

6   Grace took her black crayon and colored hard in all the empty spaces.

7   Miss Hill pinned the beautiful leaf patterns all around the room. She put the real leaves on a shelf with some acorns and horse chestnuts.

8   In a few days, the real leaves had turned dry and brown, but the leaf patterns were still bright.

9   "What a good way to keep my leaves forever!" said Grace.

1 The real leaves and the leaf patterns are alike because they both—

⬭ can be made at school with paper

⬭ turn brown after a few days

⬭ stay bright forever

⬭ can be yellow, orange, or red

2 When Grace first finds her leaves, she—

⬭ tucks them into her pocket

⬭ takes them to her teacher

⬭ makes leaf patterns

⬭ hangs them on the wall at school

3 Where does this story mostly take place?

⬭ In Grace's classroom

⬭ At Grace's house

⬭ In a forest

⬭ At the park

4 The author wrote "Autumn Treasures" to—

⬭ show that school is a fun place to make crafts

⬭ explain how leaves turn dry and brown

⬭ tell a story about a girl who makes art from nature

⬭ explain where to find the best leaves

5 What happens at the end of the story?

⬭ The real leaves turn brown.

⬭ Grace makes leaf patterns.

⬭ The leaves start to fall.

⬭ Grace finds a pretty red leaf.

GO ON ➡

3

Read the selection. Then read each question that follows it.
Decide which is the best answer to each question.
Mark the space for the answer you have chosen.

The World of Bats

1   If an animal flies, is it a bird? Not necessarily. Bats, like birds, have wings and can fly. However, bats and birds are really very different. There are about 1,000 types of bats that can be found all over the world. Most bats, though, share some common traits.

What does a bat look like?

2   Bats have a body that resembles a mouse. Their hands and arms are covered by a thin layer of skin. This allows their hands and arms to work like wings. Some bats have long tails while others do not have any tail at all. Most bats have hair that helps to keep them warm.

3   Some bats are extremely large. They can be more than five feet long from the tip of one wing to the tip of the other wing. Some bats are very small, sometimes less than two inches from one wing tip to the other.

4   Bats have two eyes and can see very well. Some bats have large eyes while others have very small eyes.

5   Bats also have two ears. They can move their ears to listen to sounds. They hear sounds very well, but they also use their hearing in other ways. They can use their hearing so they do not bump into things, and they can even use it to find their food.

6   Just like people, bats have two sets of teeth in their lifetime. They have baby teeth when they are young. As they grow up, they lose their baby teeth and grow a new set of adult teeth.

How do bats live?

7   Bats can see well even when it's dark, which means they can hunt for food at night. Bats eat a variety of things. Many bats eat bugs, while other bats eat fruit.

8   Because they search for food at night, bats usually sleep during the day. Some often sleep in caves, barns, or holes in trees. Others sleep in houses that people build for them. When a bat sleeps, it hangs upside down from its feet.

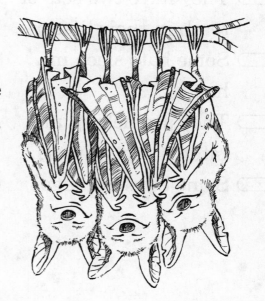

Name _____ Date _____

How do bats help people?

9   Bats help people in several ways. For example, some bats eat the bugs that bite people and destroy plants. Bats can also help people by eating fruit. After they eat the fruit, bats sometimes drop seeds. The seeds then grow into new plants.

10   Bats are very interesting and unusual animals. Not only can they fly, but they also make the world a more pleasant place for people.

---

6 Which of the following best tells how the author feels about bats?

- They have two sets of teeth in their lifetime.
- Some bats sleep in houses.
- They are helpful and interesting animals.
- Some bats eat bugs.

7 Why do bats usually sleep during the day?

- They have to sleep in caves.
- They can see very well during the day.
- They search for food at night.
- They can hang upside down only during the day.

GO ON

8 Bats help people by—

⬭ using their long tails

⬭ eating bugs that destroy plants

⬭ using their arms like wings

⬭ sleeping in barns and caves

9 All bats—

⬭ have two ears

⬭ are very large

⬭ have long tails

⬭ have small eyes

10 How do bats use their hearing?

⬭ They use their hearing to find their food.

⬭ Their hearing helps them grow new teeth.

⬭ They use their hearing to hang upside down.

⬭ Their hearing helps them destroy plants.

GO ON ➡

Name _____ Date _____

> **Read the selection. Then read each question that follows it.**
> **Decide which is the best answer to each question.**
> **Mark the space for the answer you have chosen.**

That Cat!

by Susan Campbell Bartoletti
illustrated by David LaFleur

1   Dad poked his hand into my basket. "What's that?" he asked.

2   "Mew," said the basket.

3   Dad yanked his hand away. "Oh no," he said. "Not a cat. No way."

Checkers wasn't any trouble at all—until he grew into a cat.

4   I pulled Checkers from the basket. "It's not a cat. It's a kitten. Can I keep him? Please?"

5   Dad frowned for a minute, thinking. Then he rubbed Checkers under the chin. "You'll have to take good care of him."

6   I hugged Checkers. "I will," I promised. "He won't be any trouble at all."

7   And Checkers wasn't—until he grew into a cat.

8

Name _____ Date _____

8   He wanted to be the first one *in* the house—and the first one *out* of the house. Sometimes, he tripped Dad.

9   "That cat!" Dad complained.

10   Checkers climbed onto our roof. He had no trouble getting down. Usually he aimed for Dad.

11   "That cat!" Dad hollered.

12   Checkers flushed the toilet and watched the water circle away.

13   "That cat!" Dad groaned.

14   Checkers hid in strange places. He liked to surprise people.

15   One day he hid under the couch. Dad walked by with a glass of orange juice.

16   Checkers jumped out. He curled around Dad's ankle and attacked Dad's toes. Orange juice sloshed all over the floor.

17   Dad hollered and put Checkers outside. "Scram, cat," he said. And he slammed the door.

18   Dad washed the scratches and peeled open a bandage. He wrapped it around his big toe. He opened four more for his ankle.

19   I watched from the window. Checkers looked insulted as he walked down the road.

20   "I'm sorry Checkers scratched you," I said. "He was just playing. He didn't mean to hurt you."

21   "Don't worry," said Dad. "That cat will be back."

22   After supper I called for Checkers. But Checkers didn't come.

23   Nighttime came. I called and called. I banged his food dish with a spoon. But still no Checkers.

24   I left the porch light on. But the next morning Checkers still wasn't there.

25   I carried a picture of Checkers to all the neighbors. I drew posters and hung them all over. But nobody found Checkers.

26   Days went by. Life wasn't the same without that cat.

27   I was angry with Dad. I didn't think he missed Checkers at all.

28   Then one night the phone rang. "We'll be right over," said Dad.

29   We drove to a nearby farm. The farmer opened the barn door. Out ran a black-and-white cat.

Name _____ Date _____

30   "Checkers!" I cried. I scooped him up. Checkers purred. We rubbed noses. "I missed you!" I said.

31   The farmer smiled. "Good thing I saw that ad in the paper."

32   I looked at Dad. "You put an ad in the paper?"

33   Dad's face turned red. He nodded.

34   He petted Checkers. Checkers batted at him with his paw.

35   Dad laughed. "That cat," he said. "It's good to have him back."

---

11 After Checkers runs away, Dad helps find him by—

⬭ leaving the porch light on
⬭ putting up posters
⬭ putting an ad in the paper
⬭ calling his neighbors

12 What is the main idea of this story?

⬭ It is not a good idea to have a cat as a pet.
⬭ A newspaper ad is the only way to find a lost pet.
⬭ Cats run away if their owners yell at them.
⬭ People love their pets even if their pets cause trouble.

GO ON ➡

13 Why does Checkers run away?

⬭ Dad yells at Checkers and puts him outside.

⬭ Checkers wants to live on a farm.

⬭ Dad spills orange juice on Checkers.

⬭ Checkers wants to surprise Dad.

14 At the end of the story, Dad—

⬭ wishes Checkers would run away again

⬭ is happy that they found Checkers

⬭ is sad because they cannot find Checkers

⬭ is upset and gives Checkers to the farmer

15 What can you tell about Dad from this story?

⬭ He does not want Checkers anymore.

⬭ He likes dogs more than cats.

⬭ He really wanted to find Checkers.

⬭ He is very clumsy.

GO ON ➡

> Read the selection. Then read each question that follows it.
> Decide which is the best answer to each question.
> Mark the space for the answer you have chosen.

Poison Ivy

1   Have you ever touched poison ivy? If you have, you most likely know that it can make you itch. Poison ivy is a plant that produces oil that can cause you to get a rash if you touch it or bump into it. The rash may have red bumps and blisters. It will be very itchy. It can last for several weeks.

2   It is important to know what poison ivy looks like so that you can stay away from it. It is a green plant that has leaves in groups of three. It can grow as a vine or a bush. It might be growing in the woods or in your backyard.

3   What should you do if you see that you have touched poison ivy? Tell a grown-up. Then quickly go wash any part of your skin that has touched the plant. You need to use soap and water to get the plant's oil off your skin. If you do not, you will probably start getting a rash in about ten minutes.

4   There is a rhyme about poison ivy. Leaves of three—let them be! This is good to remember.

BENCHMARK TEST

Reading

Name _____   Date _____

16 The author wrote "Poison Ivy" to—

◯ tell readers about different rashes

◯ give readers facts about poison ivy

◯ tell readers how to grow poison ivy

◯ teach readers about interesting plants

17 What should you do first if you touch poison ivy?

◯ Tell a grown-up

◯ Scratch your skin

◯ Kill the plant

◯ Wash your skin

18 What is the main idea of "Poison Ivy"?

◯ Poison ivy is a plant with three leaves.

◯ The rash from poison ivy is very itchy.

◯ Poison ivy grows in the woods.

◯ It is important to know about poison ivy.

© Houghton Mifflin Harcourt Publishing Company. All rights reserved.

14

Grade 2, Unit 1: Neighborhood Visit

Name _____ Date _____

Reading: Phonics

**Read each sentence. Then read each question that follows it.
Decide which is the best answer to each question.
Mark the space for the answer you have chosen.**

19

It was still dark when my brother told me to <u>wake</u> up.

Which word has the same vowel sound as the word <u>wake</u>?

- ⬭ splash
- ⬭ wash
- ⬭ save
- ⬭ tack

20

He <u>spoke</u> quietly so Mom wouldn't hear him.

Which word has the same vowel sound as the word <u>spoke</u>?

- ⬭ note
- ⬭ spot
- ⬭ moth
- ⬭ sock

21

We got _____ and tiptoed out of the house.

Which word is correct and best completes the sentence?

- ⬭ dessed
- ⬭ dress
- ⬭ ressed
- ⬭ dressed

22

Our <u>plan</u> was to give Mom a new garden for her birthday.

Which word has the same vowel sound as the word <u>plan</u>?

- ⬭ plane
- ⬭ late
- ⬭ dad
- ⬭ plum

GO ON ➡

Name _____ Date _____

23

We got the plants we had hidden in the <u>shed</u>.

Which word has the same vowel sound as the word <u>shed</u>?

⬭ mess
⬭ shade
⬭ dish
⬭ sale

24

Next we be<u>g</u>an digging holes for the plants.

Which word has the same sound as the underlined part of the word be<u>g</u>an?

⬭ cage
⬭ gate
⬭ gem
⬭ bridge

25

We took the plants out of their <u>pots</u> and put one in each hole.

Which word has the same vowel sound as the word <u>pots</u>?

⬭ pole
⬭ plate
⬭ drop
⬭ note

26

We watered the garden and then let Mom see our <u>gift</u>.

Which word has the same vowel sound as the word <u>gift</u>?

⬭ will
⬭ smile
⬭ I
⬭ gave

GO ON ➡

Name _____   Date _____

27

> We could tell by the look on her face that she was surprised.

Which word has the same sound as the underlined part of the word fa<u>c</u>e?

- ◯ cake
- ◯ tack
- ◯ act
- ◯ sand

28

> Mom liked her garden! She picked a red flower with white _____.

Which word is correct and best completes the sentence?

- ◯ steps
- ◯ stripes
- ◯ trips
- ◯ sips

STOP

Writing: Revising and Editing

Read the introduction and the passage that follows it. Then read each question. Decide which is the best answer to each question. Mark the space for the answer you have chosen.

Perla wrote this story about a skunk. Read Perla's story and think about how she should change it. Then answer the questions that follow.

Sam the Skunk

(1) Sam the skunk lived in a hole by a big trees. (2) He wanted to be friends with the other animals. (3) He waved at them and gav them a smile. (4) Each time he tried to move closer, the animals ran away. (5) They were afraid of Sam's smell. (6) No one wanted to be his friend.

(7) One day Sam. (8) He heard a pretty song. (9) It was Bluebird sitting in the top of his tree! (10) After she finished singing, Sam thanked her for the nice song. (11) Bluebird smiled. (12) She said she wanted to live in his tree. (13) Then she could sing for him every day.

(14) Sam asked Bluebird why his smell did not scare her. (15) Bluebird laughed. (16) She said that his smell could not reach her. (17) Way up in the treetop. (18) Sam clapped and did a little dance? (19) At last, Sam had a friend!

---

1 Look at sentence 1 again.

> (1) Sam the skunk lived in a hole by a big trees.

How should this sentence be changed?

- ⬭ Change *Sam* to **sam**
- ⬭ Change *trees* to **tree**
- ⬭ Change the period (**.**) to a question mark (**?**)

2 Look at sentence 3 again.

> (3) He waved at them and gav them a smile.

How should this sentence be changed?

- ⬭ Change *He* to **His**
- ⬭ Change *gav* to **gave**
- ⬭ Change *smile* to **smiles**

3 Look at these sentences again.

> (7) One day Sam.
>
> (8) He heard a pretty song.
>
> (11) Bluebird smiled.

Which one is **NOT** a complete sentence?

- ⬭ Sentence 7
- ⬭ Sentence 8
- ⬭ Sentence 11

4 Look at sentence 18 again.

> (18) Sam clapped and did a little dance?

How should this sentence be changed?

- ⬭ Change *little* to **Little**
- ⬭ Change *dance* to **dances**
- ⬭ Change the question mark (**?**) to a period (**.**)

5 Look at these sentences again.

> (15) Bluebird laughed.
>
> (17) Way up in the treetop.
>
> (19) At last, Sam had a friend!

Which one is **NOT** a complete sentence?

- ⬭ Sentence 15
- ⬭ Sentence 17
- ⬭ Sentence 19

GO ON ➡

Read the introduction and the passage that follows it. Then read each question. Decide which is the best answer to each question. Mark the space for the answer you have chosen.

Darius wrote this paper to tell his class about his new kite. Read Darius's paper and think about the changes he should make. Then answer the questions that follow.

A Great Kite

(1) Do you like kites (2) If you do, you will love my octopus kite! (3) It has a round head with big eyes. (4) It also has eight leg just like a real octopus. (5) My kite looks great when it flies!

(6) To fly the kite, I hold onto the string and run. (7) At first, the octopus looks flat, and it stays closs to the ground. (8) Then the wind lifts it into the air. (9) As it goes up, the head fills with air.

Name _____   Date _____

(10) First, I pull the string tight. (11) Then, little by little, the kite goes higher. (12) My octopus kite is high up in the sky. (13) The wind makes its legs move. (14) It looks like the octopus is alive. (15) It is the best kites I have ever had!

---

6   Look at sentence 1 again.

> (1) Do you like kites

How should this sentence be changed?

- ⬭ Change *you* to **You**
- ⬭ Change *kite* to **kites**
- ⬭ Put a question mark (**?**) at the end of the sentence

7   Look at sentence 4 again.

> (4) It also has eight leg just like a real octopus.

How should this sentence be changed?

- ⬭ Change *It* to **it**
- ⬭ Change *leg* to **legs**
- ⬭ Change the period (**.**) to a question mark (**?**)

GO ON

8   Look at sentence 7 again.

> (7) At first, the octopus looks flat, and it stays closs to the ground.

How should this sentence be changed?

◯ Change *first* to **last**

◯ Change *closs* to **close**

◯ Change the period (**.**) to a question mark (**?**)

9   Look at these sentences again.

> (10) First, I pull the string tight.
>
> (11) Then, little by little, the kite goes higher.
>
> (12) My octopus kite is high up in the sky.

Which word should go at the beginning of sentence 12?

◯ Finally,

◯ Before,

◯ Tomorrow,

10   Look at sentence 15 again.

> (15) It is the best kites I have ever had!

How should this sentence be changed?

◯ Change *It* to **Its**

◯ Change *kites* to **kite**

◯ Change *I* to **me**

Writing: Written Composition

> Write a true story about a time you did something that made you feel proud.

Use a separate sheet of paper to plan your composition. Then write your composition on the lined pages that follow.

The tips in the box below will help you as you write.

REMEMBER—YOU SHOULD

❏ write about a time you did something that made you feel proud

❏ give details so that the reader understands what you did and why it made you proud

❏ use complete sentences

❏ try to use correct spelling, capitalization, punctuation, and grammar

Name _____ Date _____

_____

_____

_____

_____

_____

_____

_____

_____

_____

_____

_____

_____

Name _____ Date _____

_____

_____

_____

_____

_____

_____

_____

_____

_____

_____

Reading

> **Read the selection. Then read each question that follows it.
> Decide which is the best answer to each question.
> Mark the space for the answer you have chosen.**

A New Life for Tweet

1   Tweet was a quiet little bird. All day long, he sat alone in his tree. He never sang. He just watched the world around him. Tweet watched frogs and turtles swimming in the <u>pond</u>. He watched rabbits and squirrels playing in the woods. Day after day, he sat on the same branch and watched the same things.

2   Then one day, there was something new to <u>see</u>. It happened right in Tweet's tree. Four little eggs in a nearby nest began to hatch. *Tap, tap, tap.* The baby birds used their <u>beaks</u> to crack their shells. As soon as the birds hatched, they opened their mouths wide. They were hungry! Tweet watched Mother Bird fly off to find food for them.

3   One of the babies kept trying to find its mother. It wiggled away from the other birds. Tweet got worried. The baby was very close to the edge of the nest.

4   All at once, the baby bird fell! Tweet felt <u>unsure</u> about leaving his branch, but time was running out. He flew toward the little bird with his heart <u>pounding</u>. Would he reach it in time?

5   Tweet flew as fast as he could. He swooped below the baby bird. It landed on Tweet's soft back! Then up, up, up Tweet flew. He put the little bird back in its nest.

6   Just then, Mother Bird came back with some tasty bugs for the hungry little birds. She thanked Tweet for helping her baby. To repay his kindness, she gave him the biggest, fattest bug. Tweet smiled and stood up tall. He was glad he had left his branch.

7   After that, Tweet always sat near the nest. When Mother Bird left to find food, she did not worry. Tweet's pretty song filled the forest. It let her know that her babies were safe in their nest!

GO ON

Name _____ Date _____

1 At the beginning of the story, Tweet never sings because he—

- ⬭ plays in the woods
- ⬭ sits alone in his tree
- ⬭ is afraid hunters will find him
- ⬭ doesn't want to scare the animals

2 Look at this sentence from the story again.

> Tweet watched frogs and turtles swimming in the pond.

What does the word pond mean?

- ⬭ A little creek
- ⬭ A wide river
- ⬭ A sandy beach
- ⬭ A small lake

3 Look at this sentence from the story again.

> Then one day, there was something new to see.

What does the word see mean?

- ⬭ Ocean
- ⬭ Look at
- ⬭ Hide from
- ⬭ The letter after *b*

4 Look at this sentence from the story again.

> The baby birds used their beaks to crack their shells.

What does the word beaks mean?

- ⬭ Long, sharp claws
- ⬭ Short, strong wings
- ⬭ Hard, pointed mouths
- ⬭ Loud, hungry calls

GO ON ➤

5 Tweet gets worried because he thinks—

◯ the eggs in the nest might break

◯ a baby bird might fall out of the nest

◯ the mother bird might not bring back any food

◯ squirrels might get one of the baby birds

6 Look at this sentence from the story again.

> Tweet felt <u>unsure</u> about leaving his branch, but time was running out.

What does the word <u>unsure</u> mean?

◯ Not sure

◯ Very sure

◯ Sure again

◯ Sure enough

7 Look at this sentence from the story again.

> He flew toward the little bird with his heart <u>pounding</u>.

What does the word <u>pounding</u> mean?

◯ Feeling good

◯ Standing still

◯ Watching closely

◯ Beating hard

8 How does Tweet feel when Mother Bird thanks him?

◯ Sad

◯ Tired

◯ Proud

◯ Worried

GO ON ➡

9 At the end of the story, why does Tweet sing?

⬭ To help the baby birds fall asleep

⬭ To warn other birds when there is danger

⬭ To let Mother Bird know her babies are safe

⬭ To tell the baby birds how happy he is

10 How does Tweet change by the end of the story?

⬭ He finds out that watching others is boring.

⬭ He learns that helping others makes him happy.

⬭ He understands that making friends is hard for him.

⬭ He decides being quiet will keep him out of trouble.

GO ON

Read the selection. Then read each question that follows it. Decide which is the best answer to each question. Mark the space for the answer you have chosen.

Storm Safety

Nature's Warnings

1   When the sky suddenly turns dark and the wind is strong, <u>beware</u>! A dangerous storm might be coming. Storms are scary. Watch for flashes of lightning. Listen for thunder. If nature sends these warnings, don't wait for rain. Act right away to keep safe.

Safety Steps

2   At the first flash of lightning, quickly get inside a building or a car. Do not go into a shed or <u>baseball</u> dugout. They are not closed like a building, so they are not safe.

3   Even after you are indoors, be careful. It is not smart to go near doors and windows. They can blow in or break. A room with no windows is the <u>safest</u> place to be.

4   Do not wash your hands during a storm. Do not use anything that runs on electricity either. Water and electrical lines are like roads for lightning. Even if you really want to play computer games, don't! It is better to be bored than to risk getting hurt. Try reading a book instead. Reading is more fun than playing computer games.

5   If you can't get to somewhere safe, stay out in the open. You may feel safe under a tree, but that is not a good place to be. Lightning is pulled toward tall poles and trees. Stay down low in an open space and cover your ears to protect them. Loud thunder can <u>damage</u> your hearing.

Lightning Strikes

6   Lightning does not <u>strike</u> people very often. It is not likely that you will ever see that happen. If you do, call 9-1-1. Only trained emergency workers should care for a person who has been hit by lightning.

7   If you follow these rules, you should stay safe during a storm.

GO ON

11 Look at the chart and use it to answer the question below.

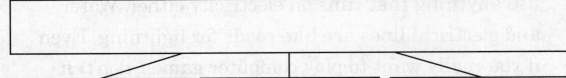

Get inside a building or car	Do not go near windows	Do not wash your hands

Which main idea belongs in the empty box?

- ⬭ What Causes Lightning
- ⬭ How to Be Safe in a Storm
- ⬭ What Emergency Workers Do
- ⬭ When Storms Happen

---

12 Look at this sentence from the article again.

> When the sky suddenly turns dark and the wind is strong, <u>beware</u>!

What does the word <u>beware</u> mean?

- ⬭ Move quick
- ⬭ Have fun
- ⬭ Stay calm
- ⬭ Watch out

13 Which is a warning that a storm is coming?

- ⬭ Dark sky
- ⬭ Open shed
- ⬭ Broken window
- ⬭ Tall poles or trees

GO ON ➡

14 Look at this sentence from the article again.

> Do not go into a shed or <u>baseball</u> dugout.

What does the word <u>baseball</u> mean?

- ⭕ A place where you start from
- ⭕ A base to build something on
- ⭕ A game that is played with a ball
- ⭕ A place to store things

15 Which sentence from the article is an opinion?

- ⭕ *Storms are scary.*
- ⭕ *Water and electrical lines are like roads for lightning.*
- ⭕ *Lightning does not strike people very often.*
- ⭕ *Do not wash your hands during storm.*

16 Look at this sentence from the article again.

> A room with no windows is the <u>safest</u> place to be.

What does the word <u>safest</u> mean?

- ⭕ Not safe
- ⭕ More safe
- ⭕ Most safe
- ⭕ In a safe way

17 Which sentence from the article is a fact?

- ⭕ *It is not smart to go near doors and windows.*
- ⭕ *It is better to be bored than to risk getting hurt.*
- ⭕ *Reading is more fun than playing computer games.*
- ⭕ *Lightning is pulled toward tall poles and trees.*

GO ON ▶

18 Look at this sentence from the article again.

> Loud thunder can <u>damage</u> your hearing.

What does the word <u>damage</u> mean?

- ⬭ Carry
- ⬭ Hurt
- ⬭ Trick
- ⬭ Surprise

19 Which section would you read to learn what to do if someone is hurt by lightning?

- ⬭ Nature's Warnings
- ⬭ Safety Steps
- ⬭ Lightning Strikes
- ⬭ Storm Safety

20 Look at this sentence from the article again.

> Lightning does not <u>strike</u> people very often.

Which word means about the same as the word <u>strike</u>?

- ⬭ Play
- ⬭ Help
- ⬭ Worry
- ⬭ Hit

Reading: Phonics

Read each sentence. Then read each question that follows it.
Decide which is the best answer to each question.
Mark the space for the answer you have chosen.

21

Chip the chipmunk was trying to _____ a best friend.

Which word is correct and best completes the sentence?

- ⬭ shoes
- ⬭ choose
- ⬭ chance
- ⬭ those

22

He had a hard time _____ on just one.

Which form of the word <u>decide</u> is correct and best completes the sentence?

- ⬭ deciding
- ⬭ decidding
- ⬭ decideing
- ⬭ deciddeing

23

Bird's sweet _____ always made him happy.

Which word is correct and best completes the sentence?

- ⬭ sonn
- ⬭ sonj
- ⬭ sogn
- ⬭ song

24

He liked to play tag with Rabbit because she was so qui<u>ck</u>.

Which word has the same sound as the underlined part of the word qui<u>ck</u>?

- ⬭ itch
- ⬭ speak
- ⬭ unit
- ⬭ nice

25 | Squirrel made him laugh when she _____ nuts in her cheeks.

Which form of the word <u>stuff</u> is correct and best completes the sentence?

○ stuffd
○ stufed
○ stuffed
○ stufffed

26 | "I just <u>can't</u> make up my mind," he thought.

What does <u>can't</u> mean in the sentence?

○ can not
○ can do
○ can't not
○ can isn't

27 | Chip _____ as he thought about each special friend.

Which form of the word <u>smile</u> is correct and best completes the sentence?

○ smileed
○ smiled
○ smild
○ smilled

28 | Suddenly, Chip shouted, "I have _____ the answer!"

Which word is correct and best completes the sentence?

○ foul
○ fang
○ fount
○ found

GO ON

Unit Test, Phonics

38

Grade 2, Unit 2: Nature Watch

29 | "I'll have three best friends," he said.

What does I'll mean in the sentence?

- ○ I would
- ○ I still
- ○ I will
- ○ I fall

30 | "Tonight, we will all eat dinner together!"

Which word rhymes with the word dinner?

- ○ diner
- ○ winner
- ○ dine
- ○ swimmer

STOP

Writing: Revising and Editing

Read the introduction and the passage that follows it. Then read each question. Decide which is the best answer to each question. Mark the space for the answer you have chosen.

Ali's class is planning a trip to a state park. He wrote these tips to help students stay safe while hiking. He wants you to help him revise and edit the paper. Read Ali's paper and think about ways he could change it to make it better. Then answer the questions that follow.

My Hiking Tips

(1) I love to hike at Bastrop State Park. (2) I think you will like it, too! (3) Here are some ways to stay safe on a hike.

(4) First, plan your hike. (5) Get a map of the park. (6) Then choose the hike that is right for you.

(7) Next, pack for safety. (8) Take a first aid kit and some water. (9) Most hikers packs a few snacks, too.

(10) Last, stay on the trails. (11) That will protect you
and the plants. (12) If you get off the trails, you can get
bug bites or scratchs. (13) You can get stuch in the mud.
(14) You can even get into poison ivy. (15) That is not fun!

(16) I hope you follow these tips. (17) If you do, you
had a great hike.

GO ON

1 Look at these sentences again.

(4) First, plan your hike. (5) Get a map of the park. (6) Then choose the hike that is right for you.

Which sentence could **BEST** be added after Sentence 5?

○ Be sure to wear good hiking shoes that fit you well.

○ Use the map to find out which trails are long or steep.

○ Taking a lot of extra things will make your pack heavy.

2 Look at sentence 9 again.

(9) Most hikers packs a few snacks, too.

How should this sentence be changed?

○ Change *hikers* to **hiker**

○ Change *packs* to **pack**

○ Change *few* to **fews**

3 Look at sentence 12 again.

(12) If you get off the trails, you can get bug bites or scratchs.

How should this sentence be changed?

○ Change *trails* to **trailes**

○ Change *bites* to **bits**

○ Change *scratchs* to **scratches**

4 Look at sentence 13 again.

(13) You can get stuch in the mud.

How should this sentence be changed?

○ Change *can* to **cann**

○ Change *get* to **got**

○ Change *stuch* to **stuck**

5 Look at sentence 17 again.

(17) If you do, you had a great hike.

How should this sentence be changed?

○ Change *had* to **has**

○ Change *had* to **will have**

○ Change the period (**.**) to a question mark (**?**)

GO ON

> **Read the introduction and the passage that follows it. Then read each question. Decide which is the best answer to each question. Mark the space for the answer you have chosen.**

Mei is in the second grade. She wrote this paper about a music camp she went to last summer. She wants you to help her revise and edit the paper. Read Mei's paper and think about the changes she should make. Then answer the questions that follow.

Camp Sing-Along

(1) Last summer I went to Camp Sing-Along. (2) We did a lot more than sing there. (3) We danced and put on plays, too!

(4) Our days were very busy. (5) We learnd new songs every morning. (6) Some were show tunes, and some were funny camp songs. (7) After lunch, group leaders taught us dance steps. (8) The first day, I kept tripping over my own fete. (9) My leader, Tanya ames, helped me

and I got a lot better. (10) At night, we acted in skits under the stars. (11) We even put on a show for our families. (12) It was awesome!

(13) Camp showed me that it can be fun to work hard. (14) Now I sing and dance every day. (15) My friend Jane takes dance lessons after school. (16) I hope I will get to star in the Camp Sing-Along show nest summer!

6   Look at sentence 5 again.

> (5) We learnd new songs every morning.

How should this sentence be changed?

- ⬭ Change *learnd* to **learned**
- ⬭ Change *songs* to **sons**
- ⬭ Change *every* to **everey**

7   Look at sentence 8 again.

> (8) The first day, I kept tripping over my own fete.

How should this sentence be changed?

- ⬭ Change *kept* to **keeped**
- ⬭ Change *own* to **one**
- ⬭ Change *fete* to **feet**

8   Look at sentence 9 again.

> (9) My leader, Tanya ames, helped me and I got a lot better.

How should this sentence be changed?

- ⬭ Change *ames* to **Ames**
- ⬭ Change *helped* to **helping**
- ⬭ Change *I* to **me**

9 Look at these sentences again.

> (3) We danced and put on plays, too!
>
> (11) We even put on a show for our families.
>
> (15) My friend Jane takes dance lessons after school.

Which sentence does **NOT** belong in this paper?

- ⬭ Sentence 3
- ⬭ Sentence 11
- ⬭ Sentence 15

10 Look at sentence 16 again.

> (16) I hope I will get to star in the Camp Sing-Along show nest summer!

How should this sentence be changed?

- ⬭ Change *will* to **while**
- ⬭ Change *Camp* to **Canp**
- ⬭ Change *nest* to **next**

Writing: Written Composition

Write instructions for playing a game you like.

Use a separate sheet of paper to plan your composition. Then write your composition on the lined pages that follow.

The tips in the box below will help you as you write.

REMEMBER—YOU SHOULD

❑ write about how to play a
   game you like

❑ make sure that each
   sentence helps the reader
   understand the rules of
   the game

❑ give enough details so that
   the reader understands
   what to do

❑ use complete sentences

❑ try to use correct spelling,
   capitalization, punctuation,
   and grammar

_____

_____

_____

_____

_____

_____

_____

_____

_____

_____

_____

_____

_____

_____

_____

_____

_____

_____

_____

_____

_____

_____

Reading

Missing Mark

by Mary Penn

illustrated by Amy Wummer

1   "Who will take me to get ice cream when you're gone?" Ashley asked. She watched her big brother, Mark, lay a shirt in his suitcase.

2   "Maybe Mom. She likes ice cream," Mark said.

3   "Who will read me stories?"

4   "Maybe Grandma. She's the best story reader in the world." Mark closed his suitcase.

5   "Who will draw me pictures?"

6   "Maybe Dad. He used to draw pictures for me," Mark said, giving Ashley a big wink. "That's it! I'm off to college!"

"Who will read me stories?"

GO ON ➡

7   "But I'll miss you!"

8   "I'll come home for visits. You know I'm leaving you in charge while I'm away. Don't let me down."

9   The next Saturday morning, the corners of Ashley's mouth drooped when she looked into Mark's empty room. He had been gone for five days, but it seemed like forever. When she slowly plodded down the stairs and into the kitchen, Mom and Dad were talking.

10   "Maybe we should take Oliver to the vet," Mom said. Mark's big beautiful dog, Oliver, was on the floor staring at the kitchen door. "He won't eat. He just lies there waiting for Mark."

11   Dad smiled at Ashley and gave her a hug. Mom poured cereal and milk into a bowl for her.

12   "You can help us in the garden after you eat, Ashley," said Mom. "We all miss Mark. If we stay busy, we won't think about it so much."

13   Ashley plopped down next to Oliver as Mom and Dad went outside. The big brown dog didn't move. His sad, hopeful eyes gazed at the door.

14   "I miss Mark, too," said Ashley, scratching his ears. Oliver looked at Ashley and whimpered.

Name _____ Date _____

15   "If you want, I'll be your new best friend. You can sleep on my bed. I won't mind at all."

16   Ashley jumped up. She got Oliver's bowl of food and set it in front of him with a clatter. Milk splashed on the floor as she carried her cereal bowl from the table. She settled next to Oliver.

17   "If you'll eat your breakfast, I'll eat mine," she said. She stuffed a spoonful of cereal in her mouth. Oliver slowly licked up the spilled milk. She put some of her cereal in Oliver's bowl. She smiled when he began munching his food.

18   Ashley put her arms around Oliver and felt much better. Being in charge was going to be a full-time job.

"If you'll eat your breakfast, I'll eat mine."

GO ON

1 Look at this sentence from the story again.

> When she slowly plodded down the stairs and into the kitchen, Mom and Dad were talking.

What does this sentence tell the reader about Ashley?

- ◯ She feels happy.
- ◯ She feels sad.
- ◯ She feels sick.
- ◯ She feels hungry.

2 What is the first thing Ashley does on Saturday morning?

- ◯ She goes into the kitchen.
- ◯ She sits down next to Oliver.
- ◯ She looks into Mark's room.
- ◯ She gives Oliver some cereal.

3 Ashley and Oliver are alike because they both—

- ◯ miss Mark
- ◯ like pictures
- ◯ eat ice cream
- ◯ like stories

4 Mark left home to—

- ◯ get a new dog
- ◯ find a job
- ◯ visit Grandma
- ◯ go to college

5 The author wrote "Missing Mark" to—

- ◯ tell a story about a girl who misses her brother
- ◯ teach readers about taking care of animals
- ◯ explain how to cheer up a friend
- ◯ show readers how to make breakfast

GO ON

Read the selection. Then read each question that follows it.
Decide which is the best answer to each question.
Mark the space for the answer you have chosen.

A Star Is Born

1   Mia Hamm was born in 1972. As a baby, she had problems with one of her feet. Her mom and dad did not know if she would ever walk or run or kick a ball, but she learned to do all of these things. Mia's parents did not know that she would grow up to be a big star, but she did. She became a soccer star!

2   Soccer is a game in which two teams play against each other. Each team has 11 players. The players cannot move the ball with their hands or arms. Each team tries to score points by kicking the ball into the goal. The winner is the team that gets the most points.

3   Mia started playing soccer when she was only 5 years old. By the time she was 15, she was such a good player that she started winning prizes. Mia loved playing the game, and people liked watching her. After she finished school, she continued to play. She played soccer games all over the world and helped her team win many games.

4   A lot of girls who watched Mia play wanted to be just like her. Mia wanted to show the girls how to have a dream and work for it, so she started teaching them how to play soccer. Now many girls love playing soccer as much as Mia does.

Name _____ Date _____

6 Why did Mia's parents think she might not ever walk or run?

- ⬭ She was very ill.
- ⬭ She had problems with her foot.
- ⬭ She was afraid.
- ⬭ She was not good at sports.

7 Mia teaches girls to play soccer because she—

- ⬭ wants to show them how to work for a dream
- ⬭ wants them to become soccer stars
- ⬭ needs more soccer players on her team
- ⬭ thinks that everyone should learn to play soccer

8 A soccer team scores a point when a player—

- ⬭ drops the ball
- ⬭ throws the ball into the goal
- ⬭ catches the ball
- ⬭ kicks the ball into the goal

9 The reader can tell that "A Star Is Born" is nonfiction because it—

- ⬭ gives facts about a real person
- ⬭ is about a soccer game
- ⬭ tells about a girl and her parents
- ⬭ is about a girl with a problem

GO ON ➡

Name _____ Date _____

> **Read the selection. Then read each question that follows it.
> Decide which is the best answer to each question.
> Mark the space for the answer you have chosen.**

How We Dare To Share

1 Do you have to share with someone at your house? I think everyone does. I know I have to share with my brother all the time. This is something we used to fight about almost every day. My brother would say that I got the bigger piece of pie. I would say that he got the bigger piece of cake.

2 Our parents did not like all of this fighting. One night our family was having some ice cream. My brother said that I had more. I said that he had more. I wanted to get a measuring cup to measure. My mother frowned. She made us put the ice cream back in the freezer until the next day.

3 Our mother and dad said that we had to find a way to solve this problem. My brother laughed and said that every time there was a larger piece of something, he should get it. I did not think that was funny at all.

Name _____ Date _____

4   I said that I was good at measuring. I could cut the pieces or get the servings and make sure they were the same size. My brother said we should take turns measuring and serving dessert. He said that would be fair.

5   Then I thought that we should take turns at something else, too. One person would get the servings. Then the other person would pick which serving he or she wanted. Now, if you are getting the servings and you know that you will get second choice, you will make sure they are the same size!

6   So now the only problem we have is remembering whose turn it is to serve and whose turn it is to pick first. I guess we will work on that problem next.

GO ON

Name _____ Date _____

10 The mother puts the ice cream back in the freezer because—

- ⬭ it is starting to melt
- ⬭ the children are fighting
- ⬭ she wants to eat it later
- ⬭ the children are not hungry

11 What is the main problem in the story?

- ⬭ The children are not good at measuring.
- ⬭ The family runs out of ice cream.
- ⬭ The brother teases his sister.
- ⬭ The children have trouble sharing.

12 After the parents tell the children to find a way to solve their problem, the children—

- ⬭ pout and leave the room
- ⬭ laugh at each other
- ⬭ think of a plan
- ⬭ eat more ice cream

13 Look at this sentence from the story again.

> My brother laughed and said that every time there was a larger piece of something, he should get it.

What does this sentence tell the reader about the brother?

- ⬭ He likes to tease his sister.
- ⬭ He wants to help his sister.
- ⬭ He is proud of his sister.
- ⬭ He is afraid of his sister.

GO ON ➡

Benchmark Test, Reading

60

Grade 2, Unit 3: Tell Me About It

> Read the selection. Then read each question that follows it.
> Decide which is the best answer to each question.
> Mark the space for the answer you have chosen.

Ben Franklin and His First Kite

written by Stephen Krensky
illustrated by Bert Dodson

1   Ten-year-old Benjamin Franklin was hard at work in his father's candle shop. He was cutting wicks. He carefully laid out each one.

2   Ben stretched his arms and let out a yawn. Candles could be tall or short, fat or thin, and even different colors. But there was nothing fun about candles for Ben.

3   "When do you think we'll be done today?" Ben asked his father.

4   "Soon enough," his father answered. "Why? Do you have special plans?"

5   Ben's father smiled.

Text and illustrations reprinted by permission of Aladdin Paperbacks, an Imprint of Simon & Schuster Children's Publishing Division.

Name _____ Date _____

6   It was a rare day indeed when Ben did not have a plan in mind.

7   "Yes," said Ben. "I want to try an experiment at the millpond."

8   "You'll be swimming, then?" his father asked.

9   Ben grinned. "Partly," he said.

10   His father nodded. Ben was a fine swimmer. That afternoon Ben flew down the streets of Boston. He was headed for home. Along the way he noticed the waves cresting in the harbor. The ships rocked back and forth. That was good, he thought. He needed a strong wind today. When Ben got to his house, his mother met him at the door. Inside, two of his sisters were busy making hasty pudding by the hearth. Ben had sixteen brothers and sisters.

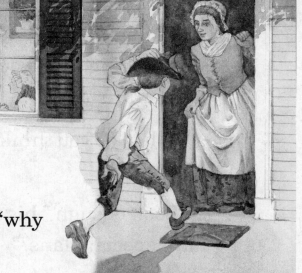

11   "Ben," his mother said, "why are you in such a hurry?"

12   Ben told her about his plan.

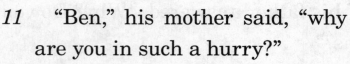

GO ON

Name _____   Date _____

13   "Since your father approves, I won't keep you," said his mother.

14   "Just be back for supper."

15   Ben nodded. He ran to get the kite he had made the week before. Then he left the house. At the millpond a few of Ben's friends had arrived to watch.

16   "You've picked a poor place to fly a kite," said one.

17   Ben shrugged. "I'm doing an experiment," he said.

18   Ben got undressed. He gave his clothes to one of his friends.

19   "Please carry these to the other side of the pond," he said.

20   "What are you going to do?" asked the other boys. "Carry the kite while you swim?"

21   "No," said Ben. "The kite is going to carry me."

22   "But that kite's nothing special. It's just paper, sticks, and strings," said one boy.

23   "That's true," Ben said. "But you see, the kite isn't the invention. The invention is what I'm going to do with it."

24   Ben raised the kite in the air. Once the wind had caught and carried it aloft, Ben walked into the water. There he lay on his back, floating.

25   "I'm going to cross this pond without swimming a stroke," said Ben.

26   The wind tugged on the kite. The kite string tightened. The water began to ripple at Ben's feet. The kite was pulling him!

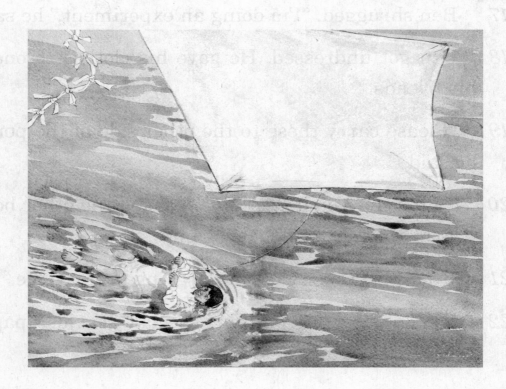

27   The boys whooped and hollered as Ben glided across the pond. Finally he reached the other side. The other boys met him there.

28   "That was amazing!" said one.

29   "You crossed the whole pond without swimming a stroke," said another.

30   "What will you do next?" they asked.

31   "Another invention?"

32   "A different experiment?"

33   Ben didn't know. But he was sure he would think of something.

---

14 Ben wants to be finished working with his father because he—

- ⬭ is sleepy
- ⬭ has plans for an experiment
- ⬭ is hungry
- ⬭ wants to play with his friends

15 The first place Ben goes after leaving his father is to—

- ⬭ the pond
- ⬭ his friend's house
- ⬭ the candle shop
- ⬭ his home

GO ON

16 Which sentence best describes Ben?

◯ He likes to try new things.

◯ He wants to make candles when he grows up.

◯ He likes making people laugh.

◯ He wants to spend more time with his family.

17 What happens after Ben gets his kite to fly?

◯ The kite falls into the water.

◯ Ben takes the kite to the pond.

◯ The kite pulls him across the pond.

◯ Ben plans his experiment.

18 Which sentence best tells what this story is about?

◯ Ben likes to do many things with his brothers and sisters.

◯ Ben works hard each day in his father's candle shop.

◯ Ben learns that candles are more important than kites.

◯ Ben finds a way to cross the pond without swimming.

Name _____ Date _____

Reading: Phonics

Read each sentence. Then read each question that follows it.
Decide which is the best answer to each question.
Mark the space for the answer you have chosen.

19

Fuzz is my <u>cute</u> little pet hamster.

Which word has the same vowel sound as the word <u>cute</u>?

- ⬭ shake
- ⬭ dust
- ⬭ used
- ⬭ coat

20

Fuzz looks like a big brown mouse without a t<u>ail</u>.

Which word has the same sound as the underlined part of the word t<u>ail</u>?

- ⬭ played
- ⬭ loaf
- ⬭ straw
- ⬭ team

21

If Fuzz gets away from me, he is very hard to ca<u>tch</u>.

Which word has the same sound as the underlined part of the word ca<u>tch</u>?

- ⬭ wash
- ⬭ rich
- ⬭ bath
- ⬭ shack

22

He plays at night and keeps me awake, so I might change his name to Fuzz the <u>Rude</u>!

Which word has the same vowel sound as the word <u>rude</u>?

- ⬭ rules
- ⬭ crust
- ⬭ opened
- ⬭ supper

GO ON ➡

Name _____   Date _____

23

> I make sure that Fuzz has everything he needs in his <u>c</u>age.

Which word has the same sound as the underlined part of the word <u>c</u>age?

- ⬭ rice
- ⬭ safe
- ⬭ king
- ⬭ chair

24

> I fill up his water bottle and sh<u>ow</u> him where the water comes out.

Which word has the same sound as the underlined part of the word sh<u>ow</u>?

- ⬭ lock
- ⬭ house
- ⬭ bond
- ⬭ float

25

> When his cage gets dirty, I <u>scr</u>ub it and line it with clean paper.

Which word has the same sound as the underlined part of the word <u>scr</u>ub?

- ⬭ scrape
- ⬭ school
- ⬭ skate
- ⬭ shrub

26

> Fuzz likes to sl<u>ee</u>p in a little toy house.

Which word has the same sound as the underlined part of the word sl<u>ee</u>p?

- ⬭ sled
- ⬭ meat
- ⬭ better
- ⬭ well

GO ON ➡

27

> I hope Fuzz <u>doesn't</u> get lonely when I'm not at home.

What does the word <u>doesn't</u> mean in the sentence?

- ⬭ do not
- ⬭ doing not
- ⬭ does not
- ⬭ did not

28

> Maybe I will get another hamster so Fuzz can have a friend!

Which word has the same sound as the underlined part of the word m<u>ay</u>be?

- ⬭ meantime
- ⬭ marked
- ⬭ lasting
- ⬭ trades

STOP

Name _____ Date _____

Writing: Revising and Editing

Read the introduction and the passage that follows it. Then read each question. Decide which is the best answer to each question. Mark the space for the answer you have chosen.

Victor wrote this paper about his favorite hobby to share with his class. Read Victor's paper and think about how he should change it. Then answer the questions that follow.

Making Model Airplanes

(1) I love making model airplanes. (2) One reason is that I learn about the past. (3) War airplanes are my favorite models. (4) To build. (5) When I build these airplanes, I read about the wars in which they were used.

(6) I also like building airplanes because it takes skill. (7) First, I work out how the pieces go together.

(8) Next, I glue the pieces in place. (9) Lastly, I paints all the details to match the real airplane. (10) I feel proud of my work when I do a good job.

(11) The best thing about building airplanes is doing it with my dad. (12) We make a great temm. (13) He teach me about all of the models. (14) We have fun choosing which ones to make. (15) We also spend hours together building the airplanes.

(16) I hope you get to build a model airplane sometime. (17) It is a lot of fun!

1   Look at sentence 2 again.

> (2) One reason is that I learn about the past.

Which sentence could **BEST** follow and support sentence 2?

⬭ I read books about all the old airplanes that I build.

⬭ I have learned to be patient and hold my hands steady.

⬭ My dad has been making models since he was my age.

2   Look at sentence 9 again.

> (9) Lastly, I paints all the details to match the real airplane.

How should this sentence be changed?

⬭ Change *paints* to **paint**

⬭ Change *match* to **matches**

⬭ Change the period (**.**) to a question mark (**?**)

3   Look at sentence 12 again.

> (12) We make a great temm.

How should this sentence be changed?

⬭ Change *We* to **we**

⬭ Change *make* to **makes**

⬭ Change *temm* to **team**

GO ON

4 Look at sentence 13 again.

(13) He teach me about all of the models.

How should this sentence be changed?

⬭ Change *He* to **he**

⬭ Change *teach* to **teaches**

⬭ Change *models* to **model**

5 Look at these sentences again.

(3) War airplanes are my favorite models.

(4) To build.

(17) It is a lot of fun!

Which one is **NOT** a complete sentence?

⬭ Sentence 3

⬭ Sentence 4

⬭ Sentence 17

GO ON

> **Read the introduction and the passage that follows it. Then read each question. Decide which is the best answer to each question. Mark the space for the answer you have chosen.**

Shelly wrote this paper about a show she put on with her friends. Read Shelly's paper and think about the changes she should make. Then answer the questions that follow.

Our Backyard Circus

(1) Last summer my friends and I put on a circus.

(2) First, we made clown suits out of old clothes. (3) Next, we made a list of jokes and tricks. (4) We worked on our acts.

(5) When the circus was ready, our families came to watch the show. (6) I told jokes. (7) One friend stood on her head. (8) Another one walked on his hands. (9) Everyone was amazed when my dog Buster jumps through a hoop.

(10) The next act made everyone laugh. (11) We wore our clown suits and rode around on tricycles. (12) I honked a silly horn, and everyone laughed. (13) Can you guess what we did next. (14) We danced and sang funny songs. (15) At the end of the show, we all bumped into each other and fell down. (16) I think that was the moost fun of all. (17) Next year, I hope that our circus will be even better?

6   Look at these sentences again.

> (2) First, we made clown suits out of old clothes.
>
> (3) Next, we made a list of jokes and tricks.
>
> (4) We worked on our acts.

What word should go at the beginning of sentence 4?

- ⬭ Finally,
- ⬭ Before,
- ⬭ Tomorrow,

7   Look at sentence 9 again.

> (9) Everyone was amazed when my dog Buster jumps through a hoop.

How should this sentence be changed?

- ⬭ Change *dog* to **Dog**
- ⬭ Change *jumps* to **jumped**
- ⬭ Change the period (**.**) to a question mark (**?**)

8   Look at sentence 13 again.

> (13) Can you guess what we did next.

How should this sentence be changed?

- ⬭ Change *Can* to **can**
- ⬭ Change *guess* to **guessing**
- ⬭ Change the period (**.**) to a question mark (**?**)

GO ON

Name _____ Date _____

9 Look at sentence 16 again.

> (16) I think that was the moost fun of all.

How should this sentence be changed?

- Change *I* to **I'm**
- Change *think* to **thinks**
- Change *moost* to **most**

10 Look at sentence 17 again.

> (17) Next year, I hope that our circus will be even better?

How should this sentence be changed?

- Change *Next* to **Last**
- Change *hope* to **hopes**
- Change the question mark **(?)** to an exclamation mark **(!)**

Name _____ Date _____

Writing: Written Composition

> Write an essay to persuade your teacher to take your class on a trip to a special place.

Use a separate sheet of paper to plan your composition. Then write your composition on the lined pages that follow.

The tips in the box below will help you as you write.

REMEMBER—YOU SHOULD

❑ write to persuade your teacher to take your class on a trip to a special place

❑ give reasons that explain why the trip is a good idea

❑ start a new paragraph for each reason

❑ use complete sentences

❑ try to use correct spelling, capitalization, punctuation, and grammar

Name _____ Date _____

79

Name _____   Date _____

_____

_____

_____

_____

_____

_____

_____

_____

_____

_____

_____

_____

Reading

> **Read the selection. Then read each question that follows it.
> Decide which is the best answer to each question.
> Mark the space for the answer you have chosen.**

Go, Rosie, Go!

1   It was another day to jump rope in gym class. Lynn and Mike turned the long rope in big, slow circles. The whole class <u>hurried</u> to get in line to wait for their <u>turn</u> to jump. Rosie stood at the back of the line and <u>frowned</u>.

2   Nick went first. He watched the rope and ran in at just the right time. Everyone counted. He made it all the way to 30 jumps. One after another, the kids watched the rope, ran in, and jumped. Then it was Rosie's turn. She watched the rope go around and around, but she didn't move. She felt like everyone was <u>staring</u> at her.

3   Rosie's friends cheered. "Go, Rosie, go!"

4   Rosie's cheeks turned red. At last, she gave it a try, but she <u>failed</u>. She tripped on the rope and fell to the ground. Rosie tried to hide the tears in her eyes.

5   Nick helped her up. "You just need some <u>practice</u>," he said in a <u>kind</u> way.

6   The truth was that Rosie had been jumping rope at home every day. With a <u>short</u> rope, she could jump 100 times without missing. She just couldn't figure out how to run in and start jumping with a long rope. Since she was the only kid on her street, there was no one to help turn the long rope.

7   Just then, Ms. Miles, the gym teacher, brought out a bunch of short jump ropes.

8   "Let's see how long each one of you can jump without missing," she said as she gave each student a short rope. "Ready, set, GO!"

9   Rosie smiled for the first time ever in gym class. As she jumped, she sang rhymes quietly to herself. Rosie tuned out the sound of all the other ropes and sneakers thumping on the ground.

10   After a while, Rosie realized that everyone was chanting. "Go, Rosie, go!"

11   She was the only one still jumping rope! The surprise almost made her miss a step, but she kept going. When at last she was too tired to go on, she stopped. The whole class <u>cheered</u>. Everyone was looking at her and smiling. Rosie smiled back!

1 At the beginning of the story, Rosie's problem is that she—

- ⬭ does not have any friends in her gym class
- ⬭ turns red because Nick makes fun of her
- ⬭ does not know the cheers that the other kids know
- ⬭ does not know how to start jumping with a long rope

2 Look at this sentence from the story again.

> The whole class <u>hurried</u> to get in line to wait for their turn to jump.

What does the word <u>hurried</u> mean?

- ⬭ Tried
- ⬭ Waited
- ⬭ Rushed
- ⬭ Pushed

3 Look at this sentence from the story again.

> Rosie stood at the back of the line and <u>frowned</u>.

Which word means the opposite of <u>frowned</u>?

- ⬭ Sat
- ⬭ Hid
- ⬭ Cried
- ⬭ Smiled

4 What happens right after Rosie trips and falls?

- ⬭ Gym class begins.
- ⬭ Nick helps Rosie get back up.
- ⬭ Everyone lines up for a turn to jump.
- ⬭ Rosie practices jumping rope at home.

GO ON ➡

5 Look at this sentence from the story again.

> She felt like everyone was <u>staring</u> at her.

What does the word <u>staring</u> mean?

- ⬭ Yelling
- ⬭ Pointing
- ⬭ Looking
- ⬭ Laughing

6 Look at this sentence from the story again.

> At last, she gave it a try, but she <u>failed</u>.

What does the word <u>failed</u> mean?

- ⬭ Did not want to
- ⬭ Was not able to
- ⬭ Changed her mind
- ⬭ Was not allowed to

7 Look at this sentence from the story again.

> "You just need some practice," he said in a <u>kind</u> way.

What does the word <u>kind</u> mean in this sentence?

- ⬭ Nice or helpful
- ⬭ One type or group
- ⬭ Alike in some way
- ⬭ Sort of or a little bit

8 Rosie smiles in gym class because she—

- ⬭ does something well at last
- ⬭ knows the class will chant for her
- ⬭ thinks that she is going to make a friend
- ⬭ has planned a surprise for her classmates

9 Use the diagram below to answer the question.

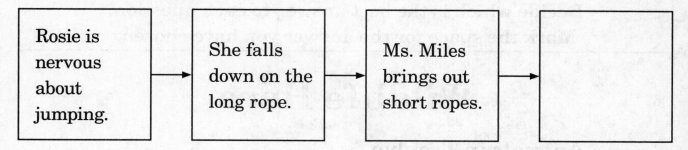

Which sentence belongs in the empty box?

◯ The class decides to play kickball.

◯ Rosie is the last one still jumping rope.

◯ Nick wins the rope-jumping contest.

◯ Rosie tries to hide in the back of the line.

---

10 How does Rosie feel when everyone looks at her once she stops jumping with the short rope?

◯ Mad

◯ Hurt

◯ Proud

◯ Foolish

GO ON

Read the selection. Then read each question that follows it.
Decide which is the best answer to each question.
Mark the space for the answer you have chosen.

Wildlife Hero

Animals in Trouble

1   Who will rescue a flying squirrel caught in a mousetrap? Who will help a snowy owl tangled in fishing line? Who will give a safe home to a bobcat with no claws? Mona Rutger—that's who! She has cared for thousands of <u>injured</u> animals. Mona runs a wildlife center in Castalia, Ohio, called Back to the Wild.

Mona's Story

2   Mona grew up on a farm. She spent a lot of time exploring the creeks and woods near the farm. She began learning about the local wildlife, too. Watching insects and animals filled her with wonder. She wanted to learn all about them.

Back to the Wild is home to a bald eagle that can't fly. The eagle flew into power lines and broke its shoulders.

3   As she got older, Mona did learn more about animals. She decided that she wanted to help

animals. She used some of her family's land to start a wildlife center. It was a place where hurt animals could live until they were ready to go back to the wild. Many people brought Mona wild animals in need of help. Some were baby animals that had lost their mothers. Others were animals that had been hit by cars. A few of the animals had eaten <u>harmful</u> chemicals. Mona helped them all.

A Hero Gets a Hand

4   Mona took care of the animals seven days a week. She didn't complain about being <u>overworked</u>, though. She knew the animals <u>depended</u> on her. In time, volunteers began to help her. Some people helped care for the animals. Others put money in a fund for the center. The fund helped pay for animal feed and medical bills. One friend wrote and told a television station about Back to the Wild. The letter led to a special award. Mona was named the <u>Hero</u> of the Year! She <u>received</u> a $10,000 prize from the television station. Mona used the money to help more animals.

5   Today, Mona is still taking care of animals. She also visits schools to teach children about protecting wild places and animals. She hopes her audiences will become heroes for animals, too!

11 Look at this sentence from the article again.

> She has cared for thousands of <u>injured</u> animals.

Which word means almost the same as <u>injured</u>?

- ⬭ Pet
- ⬭ Hurt
- ⬭ Lost
- ⬭ Fierce

12 The caption under the picture tells the reader—

- ⬭ why one eagle needed Mona's care
- ⬭ how doctors helped an injured eagle
- ⬭ why we have laws to protect bald eagles
- ⬭ why eagles like to live near cities and people

13 Which part of the article tells about Mona as a young girl?

- ⬭ The caption
- ⬭ Animals in Trouble
- ⬭ Mona's Story
- ⬭ A Hero Gets a Hand

14 The animals brought to Back to the Wild are alike because they all—

- ⬭ were hit by cars
- ⬭ are babies
- ⬭ need help
- ⬭ need to fly

GO ON ➡

15 Look at this sentence from the article again.

> A few of the animals had eaten <u>harmful</u> chemicals.

The word <u>harmful</u> means—

- ⊂⊃ harm again
- ⊂⊃ full of harm
- ⊂⊃ one who harms
- ⊂⊃ without any harm

16 How does Mona change after she opens the wildlife center?

- ⊂⊃ She no longer enjoys learning about animals.
- ⊂⊃ She starts spending every day caring for animals.
- ⊂⊃ She starts asking people to adopt wild animals as pets.
- ⊂⊃ She stops teaching children about protecting wild animals.

17 Look at this sentence from the article again.

> She didn't complain about being <u>overworked</u>, though.

The word <u>overworked</u> means—

- ⊂⊃ not worked
- ⊂⊃ able to work
- ⊂⊃ worked again
- ⊂⊃ worked too hard

18 Look at this sentence from the article again.

> She knew the animals <u>depended</u> on her.

The word <u>depended</u> means—

- ⊂⊃ loved
- ⊂⊃ needed
- ⊂⊃ watched over
- ⊂⊃ were afraid of

GO ON

19 What happens after Mona's friend writes to a television station?

⬭ Volunteers start to help Mona.

⬭ Mona closes the wildlife center.

⬭ Mona is chosen as Hero of the Year.

⬭ Mona decides to open a wildlife center.

20 Look at this sentence from the article again.

> She received a $10,000 prize from the television station.

What does the word received mean?

⬭ Got something

⬭ Gave something

⬭ Grew something

⬭ Guessed something

(STOP)

Name _____ Date _____

Reading: Phonics

Read each sentence. Then read each question that follows it.
Decide which is the best answer to each question.
Mark the space for the answer you have chosen.

21

I spent last weekend at my grandparents' f<u>ar</u>m.

Which word has the same sound as the underlined part of the word f<u>ar</u>m?

- ⬭ around
- ⬭ form
- ⬭ dark
- ⬭ grape

22

I helped Grandpa because he had a lot of h<u>ar</u>d work to do.

Which word has the same sound as the underlined part of the word h<u>ar</u>d?

- ⬭ start
- ⬭ horn
- ⬭ tray
- ⬭ care

23

While we were doing ch<u>ore</u>s, we felt a few raindrops.

Which word has the same sound as the underlined part of the word ch<u>ore</u>s?

- ⬭ frost
- ⬭ those
- ⬭ roses
- ⬭ for

24

Suddenly, the st<u>or</u>m hit and rain poured down.

Which word has the same sound as the underlined part of the word st<u>or</u>m?

- ⬭ stem
- ⬭ stone
- ⬭ shore
- ⬭ share

GO ON ➡

25

| We got soaked while we were _____ to the house. |

Which form of the word <u>run</u> is correct and best completes the sentence?

- ⬭ runing
- ⬭ ruuning
- ⬭ runnig
- ⬭ running

26

| Grandma had some dr<u>y</u> towels waiting for us. |

Which word has the same sound as the underlined part of the word dr<u>y</u>?

- ⬭ baby
- ⬭ sigh
- ⬭ clay
- ⬭ drink

27

| She _____ us to stay inside and warm up for a while. |

Which form of the word <u>want</u> is correct and best completes the sentence?

- ⬭ wantted
- ⬭ wanted
- ⬭ wantd
- ⬭ wanteed

28

| We sat by the fire and had a piece of cherry p<u>ie</u>. |

Which word has the same sound as the underlined part of the word p<u>ie</u>?

- ⬭ fry
- ⬭ pail
- ⬭ pin
- ⬭ friend

GO ON ▶

29

> I was rea<u>dy</u> to work again, so I looked out the window.

Which word has the same sound as the underlined part of the word rea<u>dy</u>?

- ⬭ dishes
- ⬭ myself
- ⬭ keeping
- ⬭ kindest

30

> The rain was gone, and a pret<u>ty</u> rainbow was in the sky!

Which word has the same sound as the underlined part of the word pret<u>ty</u>?

- ⬭ cried
- ⬭ complete
- ⬭ higher
- ⬭ prizes

Writing: Revising and Editing

Read the introduction and the passage that follows it. Then read each question. Decide which is the best answer to each question. Mark the space for the answer you have chosen.

Luisa wrote this report about barn owls to share with her class. Read Luisa's report and think about ways she could make it better. Then answer the questions that follow.

Barn Owls

(1) Barn owls is light brown birds with white faces. (2) There faces are shaped like a heart. (3) They are called barn owls because they like to live in old barns.

(4) Barn owls hunt at nite. (5) Theys eat mice and rats. (6) Soft feathers on their wings help them fly without making noise. (7) That helps them sneak up on the animals they hunt for food. (8) Barn owls use their strong claws and hooked beaks to catch their prey. (9) A bear has sharp claws because it is a hunter, too.

(10) Farmers like it when barn owls live on their farms. (11) The owls hunt the mice that eat the farmers' crops. (12) Some farmers will put wooden boxes in trees for the owls. (13) Barn owls make their homes in these boxes.

1 Look at sentence 1 again.

> (1) Barn owls is light brown birds with white faces.

How should this sentence be changed?

- ⬭ Change *is* to **are**
- ⬭ Change *light* to **lite**
- ⬭ Change *faces* to **facs**

2 Look at sentence 2 again.

> (2) There faces are shaped like a heart.

How should this sentence be changed?

- ⬭ Change *There* to **Their**
- ⬭ Change *are* to **is**
- ⬭ Change *like* to **lik**

3 Look at sentence 4 again.

> (4) Barn owls hunt at nite.

How should this sentence be changed?

- ⬭ Add a comma (**,**) after **owls**
- ⬭ Change *hunt* to **hunts**
- ⬭ Change *nite* to **night**

GO ON ➡

4   Look at sentence 5 again.

> (5) Theys eat mice and rats.

How should this sentence be changed?

○ Change **Theys** to **They**

○ Change *eat* to **ate**

○ Change the period (**.**) to a question mark (**?**).

5   Look at these sentences again.

> (6) Soft feathers on their wings help them fly without making noise.
>
> (9) A bear has sharp claws because it is a hunter, too.
>
> (11) The owls hunt the mice that eat the farmer's crops.

Which sentence does **NOT** belong in this paper?

○ Sentence 6

○ Sentence 9

○ Sentence 11

GO ON ➡

Read the introduction and the passage that follows it. Then read each question. Decide which is the best answer to each question. Mark the space for the answer you have chosen.

Andy wrote this paper about his favorite pet. Read Andy's paper and look for changes he should make. Then answer the questions that follow.

My Dog Boomer

(1) I've had some good pets, but Boomer is the best pet I've ever had. (2) He was a stray when we found him near my aunt's house in Tyler Texas. (3) Boomer was just a little puppi at the time.

(4) Now Boomer is almost as tall as I am when he stands on his hind legs. (5) He's a shaggy, white dog and has long ears.

(6) Boomer is funny. (7) When he sees a squirrel, he barks and turns in circles. (8) At the creek, he barks at dragonflies. (9) When they fly, he splashes around trying to catch them. (10) He hides whenever he sees someone wearing a hat, mittens or sunglasses.

(11) Boomer really loves me. (12) He puts his paws on my shoulders and licks my face. (13) He and me sit together while I do homework. (14) At night, he sleeps next to my bed. (15) Boomer is my best friend!

GO ON ➡

6 Look at Sentence 2 again.

(2) He was a stray when we found him near my aunt's house in Tyler Texas.

How should this sentence be changed?

⬭ Add a comma (**,**) after *Tyler*

⬭ Change *Texas* to **texas**

⬭ Change the period (**.**) to a question mark (**?**)

7 Look at Sentence 3 again.

(3) Boomer was just a little puppi at the time.

How should this sentence be changed?

⬭ Change *was* to **were**

⬭ Change *puppi* to **puppy**

⬭ Change *time* to **tim**

8 Look at these sentences again.

(4) Now Boomer is almost as tall as I am when he stands on his hind legs. (5) He's a shaggy, white dog and has long ears.

Which sentence could **BEST** be added after Sentence 5?

⬭ It has been two years since we found Boomer.

⬭ His long, wavy hair makes him look a like a big mop.

⬭ When Boomer gets scared, he hides behind Dad's chair.

GO ON

9 Look at Sentence 10 again.

> (10) He hides whenever he sees someone wearing a hat, mittens or sunglasses.

How should this sentence be changed?

- ⬭ Change *He* to **Him**
- ⬭ Change *hides* to **hide**
- ⬭ Add a comma (**,**) after **mittens**

10 Look at Sentence 13 again.

> (13) He and me sit together while I do homework.

How should this sentence be changed?

- ⬭ Change *me* to **I**
- ⬭ Change *while* to **wow**
- ⬭ Change *homework* to **home work**

Writing: Written Composition

| Write a story about planning a nice surprise for someone. |

Use a separate sheet of paper to plan your composition. Then write your composition on the lined pages that follow.

The tips in the box below will help you as you write.

REMEMBER—YOU SHOULD

❏ write about planning a nice surprise for someone

❏ give enough details so that the reader understands how you would plan the surprise

❏ use complete sentences

❏ try to use correct spelling, capitalization, punctuation, and grammar

Name _____ Date _____

_____

_____

_____

_____

_____

_____

_____

_____

_____

_____

Name _____ Date _____

_____

_____

_____

_____

_____

_____

_____

_____

_____

_____

Reading

Read the selection. Then read each question that follows it.
Decide which is the best answer to each question.
Mark the space for the answer you have chosen.

Soup and More Soup

1 "Grandma is coming for a visit," Dad said. "Let's make something special to eat."

2 "I know just what we should make," said Sophia. "Grandma gave us a <u>recipe</u> for her delicious white bean soup. Let's surprise her with that."

3 Marcos said that soup was his favorite, and Dad agreed that the bean soup was a great idea. Dad found the recipe and said, "We need to start with two cups of beans. That doesn't sound like very much. It must mean two cups for each person. If we want to make soup for four people, then how many cups of beans will we need?"

4 "Eight!" Sophia and Marcos shouted at the same time. They both loved to solve math problems.

5   Dad laughed. Then they figured out how many tomatoes, carrots, and cups of water they would need for four servings.

6   Dad, Sophia, and Marcos took turns adding the items to the soup pot.

7   Sophia said, "I think we're going to need a bigger pot!"

8   Dad found a bigger pot. "This is a lot of soup," he said.

9   Dad read the recipe again. At the bottom of the page, Grandma had written that the recipe made enough for four servings. Dad had not seen that the first time he read the recipe. He explained what had happened to Sophia and Marcos. "What is four times four?" he asked.

10   "Sixteen!" they both answered.

11   "So we have enough soup for sixteen people," Dad said.

12   Sophia knew just what to do. When Grandma rang the doorbell, all their neighbors were waiting in the backyard to visit with Grandma, too!

GO ON

1 Marcos's favorite food is—

◯ beans

◯ carrots

◯ tomatoes

◯ soup

2 Which word describes how Marcos and Sophia feel about Grandma's visit?

◯ Sad

◯ Nervous

◯ Excited

◯ Sleepy

3 Look at this sentence from the story again.

> Grandma gave us a recipe for her delicious white bean soup.

Which word means almost the same as recipe?

◯ Spoon

◯ Ideas

◯ Soup pot

◯ Directions

4 Both Marcos and Sophia—

◯ are good at math

◯ visit Grandma often

◯ are the same age

◯ invite the neighbors

GO ON

**Read the selection. Then read each question that follows it.
Decide which is the best answer to each question.
Mark the space for the answer you have chosen.**

The Potato's Path

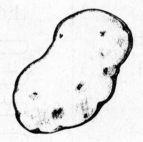

1   I love to eat potatoes.
       Yum, yum, yum, yum, yum!
       But when I eat potatoes,
       I wonder where they're from.

2   Do they drop down from the air
       Or wash in from the sea?
       My brain keeps asking where,
       So Mom sat down and told me.

3   "Potatoes come from far away,
       From a farm out on the plain.
       The farmer picks them every day
       And puts them on a train.

4   They ride the train all day and night,
    And when the sun comes up,
    A team of workers use all their might
    And load them on a truck.

5   The spuds are driven through the town
    And to the grocer's door.
    The grocer weighs them to the pound
    And puts them in the store."

6   Potatoes make me happy!
    I know just where they're from.
    They've made a long, hard journey
    To travel to our home.

5 Look at these sentences from the poem again.

> The spuds are driven through the town
> And to the grocer's door.
> The grocer weighs them to the pound
> And puts them in the store.

A grocer is someone who—

- ⬭ sells food
- ⬭ grows potatoes
- ⬭ drives a truck
- ⬭ likes to shop

6 Potatoes start their journey—

- ⬭ at the store
- ⬭ in a train
- ⬭ on a farm
- ⬭ on a truck

7 Another word for "potato" that is used in the poem is—

- ⬭ worker
- ⬭ yum
- ⬭ spud
- ⬭ team

8 What probably happens after the grocer puts the potatoes in the store?

- ⬭ The grocer sends them back to the farm.
- ⬭ Workers put them a train.
- ⬭ They get loaded onto another truck.
- ⬭ Someone buys them.

GO ON

> **Read the selection. Then read each question that follows it.
> Decide which is the best answer to each question.
> Mark the space for the answer you have chosen.**

Who's Home in Prairie Dog Town?

by Catherine Ripley

1   It's a busy morning in prairie dog town.

2   "Grrr! Grrrr!" argue two black-tailed prairie dog brothers, grinding their teeth. Close by, Mom nibbles and cleans their sister's short fur while a cousin dig, dig, digs a hole. Farther away, Auntie snacks on a blade of buffalo grass.

3   "Chirk, chirk!" warns Dad, who has spotted a golden eagle high in the sky. All across town, prairie dogs watch the eagle and chirk to alert others who have not seen it. When the eagle swoops lower, Dad announces the danger loudly. "CHIRK!" In a flash, the prairie dog families dive into their burrows. They wait safely underground for the eagle to fly away.

GO ON ➡

4   Prairie dogs use their long, curved claws to dig lots of escape holes, so they will always have safe spots to hide. They also dig large, deep tunnels to live in. At the front door of their homes, they mound up the earth. The small hill makes a great lookout tower! Just inside the tunnel, there is usually a room where a prairie dog can listen for danger but remain hidden. Deeper down is a nesting room for babies and maybe a sleeping room. All the homes have a back door. After all, some <u>predators</u>, such as black-footed ferrets, sneak into the tunnels to hunt prairie dogs. It's only smart to have more than one way out!

5   Prairie dog tunnels stay warm in the freezing winter and cool in the hot summer. They help improve the soil on the dry prairie too. All that digging loosens the earth, allowing rain to seep in more deeply.

Each family of prairie dogs has its own burrow. These are lots of families in the town, which can cover miles of open prairie.

GO ON

6   Prairie dogs don't just dig and dig. They eat and eat. Their nibbling keeps the tall grasses clipped short. Trimming the grass keeps it fresh and nutritious, and makes room for other kinds of plants to grow. The variety of plants in prairie dog town attracts many different kinds of animals.

Yum, yum!

7   Antelope and bison often drop by to munch on the young, tender grass. Sometimes a bison will take a dust bath. It rolls around in the short grass and dirt to rub off the itchy pests on its back. The plants growing in prairie dog town also attract many insects, and the insects in turn attract the birds, mice, and lizards that eat them.

8   So, prairie dog town is home to lots of animals, not just prairie dogs. Rattlesnakes, burrowing owls, and rabbits even use abandoned prairie dog burrows for their homes.

GO ON

9   Without all the nibbling and digging by prairie dogs, the prairie would be much less lively and healthy. And less noisy, too!

10   Mom pokes her head out of her front door. Has the eagle gone? Yes! Up she jumps. Leaning backward, she lets out a yip. "WEEE-OH!" Other heads poke out of burrows, and soon the two prairie dog brothers are back, arguing, tumbling, and playing across the prairie.

GO ON

9 Look at this sentence from the article again.

> After all, some <u>predators</u>, such as black-footed ferrets, sneak into the tunnels to hunt prairie dogs.

Which word means almost the same as <u>predators</u>?

- ⬭ Hunters
- ⬭ Friends
- ⬭ Family
- ⬭ Rabbits

10 At the beginning of the article, Mom is—

- ⬭ grinding her teeth
- ⬭ snacking on a blade of grass
- ⬭ digging a hole
- ⬭ cleaning her child's fur

11 Prairie dogs need lookout towers—

- ⬭ so they can stay warm
- ⬭ to spot trouble
- ⬭ so they can dig deep tunnels
- ⬭ to help the grass grow

12 Look at the pictures in the article. How do prairie dogs eat?

- ⬭ They use their strong tails to pull up the tall grass.
- ⬭ They eat in the water.
- ⬭ They use their hands to bring food to their mouths.
- ⬭ They lie down to eat.

13 If an enemy crawled into a prairie dog's tunnel, the prairie dog would probably—

- ⬭ take a dust bath
- ⬭ climb into the nesting room
- ⬭ dig a bigger hole
- ⬭ run out the back door

GO ON ➡

Read the selection. Then read each question that follows it.
Decide which is the best answer to each question.
Mark the space for the answer you have chosen.

Zachary's Feather

by Virginia S. Baldridge
art by Helen Cogancherry

1   One day when Zachary was visiting his grandpa and grandma, he found something on the grass.

2   "Look, Grandpa, a bird lost a pretty white feather," he said.

3   "Might be from a chicken," Grandpa said, "because it's so big. Put it in your cap and you can be Yankee Doodle."

4   But Zachary wasn't listening. He was running back to the kitchen.

5   "Grandma, Grandma," he called. "I need a glass of water!"

6   "Are you thirsty?" asked Grandma, getting a glass from the cupboard.

7   Zachary dragged the kitchen stool over to the sink and climbed up. "I can do it," he said. He filled the glass with water.

8   "It's not for me," he told Grandma. He put the feather carefully into the glass of water and climbed down.

9   That night, after he had taken his bath and Grandma had read three stories to him, Zachary fell asleep. He dreamed that his feather sent down white tangled roots inside the glass, like the ivy his mother grew in water. From the top of the feather grew a beautiful feather vine, curling upward, branching out with soft downy tendrils, and stirring in the breeze from the open kitchen window.

10   In the morning, Zachary ran downstairs to see his feather vine. But the feather was sticking in the glass of water just as he left it.

11   After breakfast, Zachary took his feather outside and planted it in the flower garden.

12   That night he closed his eyes and dreamed of a tall, straight, feather tree, with many branches spreading out to shade the lawn, each branch covered with fluffy feather leaves, shining in the sunlight and swaying in the breeze.

13   After two days the feather was still the same, only dirtier. Zachary washed and dried the feather. "I want to use my feather for something," he said fiercely.

14   "You could stick it in your baseball cap," Grandma said. Zachary shook his head. All morning, Zachary carried his feather around, thinking and thinking.

15   When he got up from his nap that afternoon, it was raining. "How would you like to paint some pictures?" Grandma asked, spreading newspapers over the kitchen table and getting some small jars of red, blue, and yellow paint.

16   "Oh, Grandma, oh, Grandma! Not a picture, no, not a picture!" Zachary exclaimed. "But I know how to use my feather!"

17   So Zachary sat at the table and, with some help from his grandma, he used his feather. He dipped it into the red paint and made a letter for his parents.

Dear Mommy and Daddy
I found a feather. It writes.
Love, Zachary

Name _____ Date _____

14 At the beginning of the story, why doesn't Zachary listen to Grandpa?

- ⬭ Zachary is too excited.
- ⬭ Grandpa speaks too quietly.
- ⬭ Grandpa is being silly.
- ⬭ Zachary is busy writing a letter.

15 What happens in Zachary's first dream?

- ⬭ Zachary plants the feather in the garden.
- ⬭ The feather becomes a vine.
- ⬭ Zachary puts the feather in a glass of water.
- ⬭ The feather becomes a tree.

16 If Zachary found a beautiful leaf on the ground, he would probably—

- ⬭ throw it away
- ⬭ give it to his Grandpa
- ⬭ leave it where he found it
- ⬭ do something creative with it

17 The story takes place—

- ⬭ at Zachary's grandparents' house
- ⬭ in Zachary's school
- ⬭ at Zachary's friend's house
- ⬭ in Zachary's dream

Reading: Phonics

Read each sentence. Then read each question that follows it.
Decide which is the best answer to each question.
Mark the space for the answer you have chosen.

18 | I like to daydream about life in the _____.

Which word is correct and best completes the sentence?

- ⬭ future
- ⬭ futhure
- ⬭ futer
- ⬭ futhe

19 | I'm sure there will be all kinds of _____ inventions.

Which form of the word <u>help</u> is correct and best completes the sentence?

- ⬭ helpful
- ⬭ helps
- ⬭ helped
- ⬭ helpping

20 | Robots may s<u>er</u>ve people their meals.

Which word has the same sound as the underlined part of the word s<u>er</u>ve?

- ⬭ bark
- ⬭ deer
- ⬭ more
- ⬭ hurt

21 | Machines might cl<u>ea</u>n a house at the flip of a switch.

Which word has the same sound as the underlined part of the word cl<u>ea</u>n?

- ⬭ plan
- ⬭ spend
- ⬭ trees
- ⬭ rake

GO ON ➡

Name _____ Date _____

22

> Maybe people will use their
> voices to _____ and open doors.

Which word is correct and
best completes the sentence?

- ⬭ prelock
- ⬭ unlock
- ⬭ overlock
- ⬭ mislock

23

> Cars could even have giant
> wings to fly over traffic jams!

Which word has the same
sound as the underlined part
of the word giant?

- ⬭ gate
- ⬭ night
- ⬭ sing
- ⬭ jelly

24

> I _____ kids in the future will
> have a lot of fun.

Which word is correct and
best completes the sentence?

- ⬭ thing
- ⬭ think
- ⬭ thick
- ⬭ thin

25

> They might use jet shoes to
> run high in the sky!

Which word has the same
sound as the underlined part
of the word high?

- ⬭ kite
- ⬭ pig
- ⬭ with
- ⬭ hay

GO ON ➤

Name _____ Date _____

26 | Jet shoes would make it easy to sc<u>ore</u> in basketball, too.

Which word has the same sound as the underlined part of the word sc<u>ore</u>?

- ⬭ scare
- ⬭ about
- ⬭ story
- ⬭ flower

27 | I wish we were in the future <u>a</u>lready!

Which word has the same sound as the underlined part of the word <u>a</u>lready?

- ⬭ whale
- ⬭ crawl
- ⬭ pal
- ⬭ share

(STOP)

Writing: Revising and Editing

Read the introduction and the passage that follows it. Then read each question. Decide which is the best answer to each question. Mark the space for the answer you have chosen.

Mia read a book about the brain. She wrote this report to tell what she learned. Read Mia's report and think about how she should change it. Then answer the questions that follow.

What Your Brain Does

(1) The human brain has different parts. (2) A biggest part is used for thinking. (3) It help you read books, draw, and solve problems. (4) You also use it to remember things. (5) Without this part of your brain, you would froget everything!

(6) Another part of your brain is the boss of your muscles. (7) When your brain knows you want to run or swim, it starts giving orders. (8) It tells your arm and leg muscles to move. (9) Then it sends messages so your muscles will work together. (10) If your brain didn't do its job, all of the parts would not move at the right time.

(11) Another part of your brain are called the stem. (12) It is small, but it does a big job. (13) It tells your heart to beat! (14) It also makes sure that you breathe. (15) Your brain keeps working even when you sleep. (16) Its work is never done!

1 Look at sentence 2 again.

(2) A biggest part is used for thinking.

How should this sentence be changed?

- ⬭ Change *A* to **The**
- ⬭ Change *for* to **four**
- ⬭ Change the period (**.**) to a question mark (**?**)

2 Look at sentence 3 again.

(3) It help you read books, draw, and solve problems.

How should this sentence be changed?

- ⬭ Change *help* to **helps**
- ⬭ Change *read* to **reed**
- ⬭ Change *problems* to **problem**

3 Look at sentence 5 again.

(5) Without this part of your brain, you would froget everything!

How should this sentence be changed?

- ⬭ Change *you* to **you've**
- ⬭ Change *froget* to **forget**
- ⬭ Change the exclamation mark (**!**) to a question mark (**?**)

4 Look at these sentences again.

> (7) When your brain knows you want to run or swim, it starts giving orders.
>
> (8) It tells your arm and leg muscles to move.
>
> (9) Then it sends messages so your muscles will work together.

What word should go at the beginning of sentence 8?

◯ Finally,

◯ First,

◯ Later,

5 Look at sentence 11 again.

> (11) Another part of your brain are called the stem.

How should this sentence be changed?

◯ Change *your* to **you're**

◯ Change *are* to **is**

◯ Change *called* to **calling**

Read the introduction and the passage that follows it. Then read each question. Decide which is the best answer to each question. Mark the space for the answer you have chosen.

Jason wrote this story about a trip to the lake. Read Jason's story and think about the changes he should make. Then answer the questions that follow.

Fun at the Lake

(1) My cousins and I went swimming. (2) My aunt set up a big umbrella with a stand. (3) She sat undr it and watched us from the shade.

(4) Suddenly, a big wind started blowing. (5) It lifted the umbrella up into the sky! (6) When the wind stopped, the umbrella landed upside down in a tree.

(7) My cousins and I ran to help. (8) First, we tried to reach the umbrella with long sticks. (9) The sticks we

Name _____ Date _____

found weren't long enough. (10) We came up with a new plan. (11) We patted wet sand into small balls. (12) It was like a funny kind of basketball game!

(13) Each time a sand ball landed in the umbrella, it dropped a little. (14) Finally, it crashed to the ground. (15) My aunt sayed our idea was clever.

(16) My cousins and I wished the umbrella hadn't fallen down so soon. (17) It was fun playing sand basketball!

6 Look at these sentences again.

> (1) My cousins and I went swimming.
>
> (2) My aunt set up a big umbrella with a stand.

Which sentence could **BEST** be added before sentence 1?

⬭ I am the best swimmer in my family.

⬭ Last summer I went to the lake with my cousins.

⬭ On Saturdays, I have to do my chores before I can go outside.

7 Look at sentence 3 again.

> (3) She sat undr it and watched us from the shade.

How should this sentence be changed?

⬭ Change **She** to **I**

⬭ Change **undr** to **under**

⬭ Change **the** to **an**

8 Look at these sentences again.

> (8) First, we tried to reach the umbrella with long sticks.
>
> (9) The sticks we found weren't long enough.
>
> (10) We came up with a new plan.

Which word should be added at the beginning of sentence 10?

⬭ First

⬭ While

⬭ Then

GO ON ➡

Name _____ Date _____

9 Look at these sentences again.

> (11) We patted wet sand into small balls.
>
> (12) It was like a funny kind of basketball game!

Which sentence could **BEST** be added after sentence 11?

- ⬭ We decided we would have a swimming race after lunch.
- ⬭ My cousins thought that digging in the sand was a lot of fun.
- ⬭ We threw the balls and tried to make them land in the umbrella.

10 Look at sentence 15 again.

> (15) My aunt sayed our idea was clever.

How should this sentence be changed?

- ⬭ Change *sayed* to **said**
- ⬭ Change *was* to **were**
- ⬭ Change the period (**.**) to a question mark (**?**)

Writing: Written Composition

> Write to tell some of the important things you know about staying strong and healthy. You may need to write more than one paragraph.

Use a separate sheet of paper to plan your composition. Then write your composition on the lined pages that follow.

The tips in the box below will help you as you write.

REMEMBER—YOU SHOULD

❑ write to tell some things you know about staying strong and healthy

❑ start each paragraph with one important idea about staying strong and healthy

❑ give enough details so that the reader understands how to stay strong and healthy

❑ use complete sentences

❑ try to use correct spelling, capitalization, punctuation, and grammar

---

Name _____ Date _____

_____

_____

_____

_____

_____

_____

_____

_____

_____

_____

_____

Name _____ Date _____

_____

_____

_____

_____

_____

_____

_____

_____

_____

_____

Reading

Read the selection. Then read each question that follows it. Decide which is the best answer to each question. Mark the space for the answer you have chosen.

Good Boy, Buster!

1   One sunny autumn day, Gabby and her dad were in the backyard, playing with their dog, Buster. Gabby <u>tossed</u> the ball for Buster. "Go get it!" she cried.

2   Then Buster <u>noticed</u> a cardinal and scampered after it. "Come back here, Buster!" Gabby called.

3   Dad tried, too. "Buster, behave! Come back!" Buster looked at them and wagged his tail, but he did not come.

4   "What a naughty dog we have," Gabby sighed. "He never obeys, and he always jumps on me and barks!"

5   "Don't be upset," said Dad. "He's a nice dog but he needs some training."

6   The following day, Gabby and Dad went to the library. They checked out a book that <u>explained</u> how to train dogs. Together they read the chapter about

teaching a dog to come when called. "This sounds sensible," said Dad. "I think it will work."

7   "I can't wait to try it," Gabby replied.

8   When they got home from the library, Buster jumped up and down, wagging his tail. Dad said, "Okay, Buster, we've got work to do!"

9   Dad and Gabby followed the <u>steps</u> in the book exactly. Gabby held a small treat in her hand. In a firm voice she said, "Buster, come." The moment Buster looked at her, she smiled and praised him. "Good boy!" she chirped. As Buster walked toward her, she continued smiling and talking to him. As soon as he reached her, she rewarded him with the treat.

10   Dad tried it next. This time, Buster came to Dad a little faster. Dad grinned. "He's off to a good start!"

11   Gabby and Dad practiced with Buster every afternoon. After a week, they tried teaching Buster to sit. Buster looked <u>confused</u> at first, but soon he was sitting every time they gave him the command.

12   Over the course of only a few weeks, Buster had learned to come, sit, and lie down. Dad scratched Buster's ears and said, "I'm proud of you!"

13   Gabby stroked Buster's back. "I'm sorry I said you were a naughty dog. You're a terrific dog!"

14   Buster didn't jump up, and he didn't bark. He just listened and wagged his tail!

GO ON

Name _____ Date _____

1 Look at this sentence from the story again.

> Gabby <u>tossed</u> the ball for Buster.

What does the word <u>tossed</u> mean?

- ⬭ Rolled
- ⬭ Caught
- ⬭ Threw
- ⬭ Bounced

2 At the beginning of the story, Dad is different from Gabby because he—

- ⬭ thinks Buster is nice
- ⬭ does not want Buster to come
- ⬭ does not enjoy playing with Buster
- ⬭ thinks it is funny when Buster chases a bird

3 Read the meanings below for the word <u>notice</u>. Then look at the sentence from the story again.

> **notice** \nō tis\
> *verb*
> 1. to see
> 2. to comment on
> *noun*
> 3. an announcement
> 4. a poster making an announcement

> Then Buster <u>noticed</u> a cardinal and scampered after it.

Which meaning best fits the way <u>noticed</u> is used in this sentence?

- ⬭ Meaning 1
- ⬭ Meaning 2
- ⬭ Meaning 3
- ⬭ Meaning 4

GO ON ➤

4 What is the main problem in this story?

- ⬭ Buster must learn to sit.
- ⬭ Buster does not behave.
- ⬭ Gabby does not like Buster.
- ⬭ Dad and Gabby must get a book.

5 Look at this sentence from the story again.

> They checked out a book that <u>explained</u> how to train dogs.

The word <u>explained</u> means—

- ⬭ gave a test
- ⬭ gave prizes
- ⬭ gave a treat
- ⬭ gave information

6 How does Gabby feel when she and Dad get the book at the library?

- ⬭ Upset
- ⬭ Proud
- ⬭ Excited
- ⬭ Worried

7 Look at this sentence from the story again.

> Dad and Gabby followed the <u>steps</u> in the book exactly.

What does the word <u>steps</u> mean in this sentence?

- ⬭ Stairs
- ⬭ Walks
- ⬭ Parts of a dance
- ⬭ Parts that tell how to do something

GO ON

8 Look at this sentence from the story again.

> Buster looked <u>confused</u> at first, but soon he was sitting every time they gave him the command.

The word <u>confused</u> means—

- ⬭ angry
- ⬭ thankful
- ⬭ not sure
- ⬭ not happy

9 By the end of the story, Gabby has changed because she—

- ⬭ enjoys giving Buster treats
- ⬭ thinks Buster is a good dog
- ⬭ learns that dogs do not always behave
- ⬭ knows that training dogs does not work

10 Use the chart below to answer the question.

Beginning of the story	Buster does not come when he is called.
Middle of the story	Dad and Gabby read a book about training dogs.
End of the story	

Which event belongs in the empty box?

- ⬭ Buster chases a cardinal.
- ⬭ Gabby and Dad go to the library.
- ⬭ Gabby tosses the ball for Buster.
- ⬭ Buster learns to sit, come, and lie down.

Read the selection. Then read each question that follows it. Decide which is the best answer to each question. Mark the space for the answer you have chosen.

The Johnson Space Center: Linking Earth to Space

1   The space shuttle orbits Earth. Inside, a crew of astronauts is hard at work. One astronaut flies the shuttle. Another repairs a broken part. Other astronauts check the computers. A team does a science experiment. Together, they keep the shuttle running, but they could not do it without help from below! Back on Earth, people at the Johnson Space Center in Houston, Texas, help keep the shuttle going.

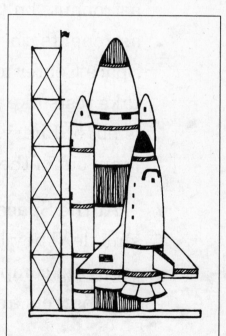

The space shuttle, soon to be retired, is carried by rockets.

2   The Mission Control Center is an important part of the Johnson Space Center. Some might call it the "brains" of the space shuttle. It is also a great place to work. Teams of 50 people keep an eye on everything

the shuttle crew does. People at Mission Control watch all of the computers on the shuttle. When a problem comes up, they help the shuttle crew solve it. The crew is <u>grateful</u> for the people who work at Mission Control. They are the best!

3   In a way, Johnson Space Center is "home" for all the astronauts on the shuttle. <u>Before</u> people can become astronauts, they must work hard. They train at the Space Center for 20 months. They must study and take tests like ordinary students. Some of their work is not ordinary. They learn to fly planes and how to <u>jump</u> out of them!

4   At the Space Center, students learn all about the shuttle. They learn what makes it fly. The students study its computers and radios. They practice using the controls and putting on the space suits.

5   The Space Center will stop using the shuttle soon. They have more exciting plans for the future! They have designed a new spaceship. In the <u>future</u>, it will take people to the moon. One day, they will use it to travel to Mars.

GO ON

Name _____ Date _____

6   The new spaceship does not hold as many people as the shuttle. Only six astronauts can travel in it, but it can stay in space for much longer. Who will the six astronauts be? If you train at the Space Center, one of them might be you!

---

11 Look at this sentence from the article again.

> The crew is <u>grateful</u> for the people who work at Mission Control.

The word <u>grateful</u> means full of—

  ◯ help

  ◯ need

  ◯ thanks

  ◯ problems

12 Which sentence from the article is an opinion?

  ◯ *A team does a science experiment.*

  ◯ *It is also a great place to work.*

  ◯ *Teams of 50 people keep an eye on everything the shuttle crew does.*

  ◯ *The Space Center will stop using the shuttle soon.*

13 The article includes a picture that shows the reader what—

⬯ the space shuttle looks like

⬯ astronauts do at the Space Center

⬯ astronauts do on the space shuttle

⬯ the Mission Control Center looks like

14 Look at this sentence from the article again.

> Before people can become astronauts, they must work hard.

Which word means the opposite of the word before?

⬯ Until

⬯ When

⬯ Never

⬯ After

15 Children in school and astronauts at the Johnson Space Center are alike because they both—

⬯ take tests

⬯ wear space suits

⬯ learn to jump out of planes

⬯ learn to use the shuttle controls

16 Look at this sentence from the article again.

> They learn to fly planes and how to jump out of them!

Which word means about the same thing as jump?

⬯ Fall

⬯ Run

⬯ Roll

⬯ Leap

GO ON ▶

17 Which sentence about the article is a fact?

○ Astronauts are the best!

○ Astronauts enjoy doing a lot of hard work.

○ The Space Center plans are exciting.

○ The space shuttle is carried by rockets.

18 Look at this sentence from the article again.

In the <u>future</u>, it will take people to the moon.

What does the word <u>future</u> mean?

○ The time that is here now

○ The time that will come later

○ The time that is remembered

○ The time that has already happened

19 How is the new spaceship different from the space shuttle?

○ The new spaceship is slower.

○ The new spaceship holds more people.

○ The new spaceship can stay in space longer.

○ The new spaceship has already been to Mars.

20 Which word names a group of people?

○ Crew

○ Astronaut

○ Mission

○ Shuttle

STOP

Reading: Phonics

> **Read each sentence. Then read each question that follows it.**
> **Decide which is the best answer to each question.**
> **Mark the space for the answer you have chosen.**

21

> Jim and Jan went swimming at the p<u>oo</u>l last week.

Which word has the same sound as the underlined part of the word p<u>oo</u>l?

- ⬭ bone
- ⬭ mouth
- ⬭ soup
- ⬭ hop

22

> Jan wore her <u>new</u> bathing suit.

Which word has the same sound as the underlined part of the word n<u>ew</u>?

- ⬭ throw
- ⬭ tree
- ⬭ fly
- ⬭ clue

23

> "The water l<u>oo</u>ks cold," she said.

Which word has the same sound as the underlined part of the word l<u>oo</u>ks?

- ⬭ stood
- ⬭ gown
- ⬭ noon
- ⬭ float

24

> Jim put his <u>foo</u>t in the water.

Which word has the same sound as the underlined part of the word f<u>oo</u>t?

- ⬭ crew
- ⬭ put
- ⬭ rope
- ⬭ group

25

> He fr<u>ow</u>ned and said, "Yes, it is chilly!"

Which word has the same sound as the underlined part of the word fr<u>ow</u>ned?

- ⬯ round
- ⬯ soon
- ⬯ boat
- ⬯ saw

26

> "Let's c<u>ou</u>nt to three and jump in," said Jan.

Which word has the same sound as the underlined part of the word c<u>ou</u>nt?

- ⬯ up
- ⬯ owl
- ⬯ ice
- ⬯ on

27

> "I can jump h<u>igh</u>er than you!" laughed Jim.

Which word has the same sound as the underlined part of the word h<u>igh</u>er?

- ⬯ treat
- ⬯ big
- ⬯ train
- ⬯ nice

28

> Jim jumped in, spr<u>ay</u>ing water on Jan.

Which word has the same sound as the underlined part of the word spr<u>ay</u>ing?

- ⬯ team
- ⬯ might
- ⬯ wait
- ⬯ cat

GO ON

29 | Jan got in the water sl<u>ow</u>ly.

Which word has the same sound as the underlined part of the word sl<u>ow</u>ly?

- ⬭ soap
- ⬭ through
- ⬭ boot
- ⬭ lock

30 | The water was not r<u>ea</u>lly cold after all.

Which word has the same sound as the underlined part of the word r<u>ea</u>lly?

- ⬭ mate
- ⬭ meet
- ⬭ bed
- ⬭ crab

STOP

Writing: Revising and Editing

> **Read each introduction and the passage that follows it. Then read each question. Decide which is the best answer to each question. Mark the space for the answer you have chosen.**

Kayla is in the second grade. She wrote this paper about her cat. She wants you to help her revise and edit the paper. Read it and think about what changes Kayla should make. Then answer the questions that follow.

My Cat

(1) I have a little cat named Meow. (2) I take care of her and fix her dinner every day. (3) My little brother wants to take care of her, but he isnt old enough. (4) He is only three years old. (5) I let him help me feed her sometime, and that makes him happy.

(6) I love playing with my cat. (7) Meows' favorite toy is a feather on a stick. (8) I shake it back and forth and she chases it. (9) She also has a little toy mose on a string. (10) I move it around, and Meow watches it quiet. (11) Then she jumps on it and bites it!

(12) When Meow gets tired, she likes to curl up on my bed. (13) Then I pet her soft fur and she goes to sleep purring.

GO ON

1 Look at sentence 3 again.

> (3) My little brother wants to take care of her, but he isnt old enough.

How should this sentence be changed?

- ⬭ Change **My** to **Mine**
- ⬭ Change **isnt** to **isn't**
- ⬭ Change **old** to **oldest**

2 Look at sentence 5 again.

> (5) I let him help me feed her sometime, and that makes him happy.

How should this sentence be changed?

- ⬭ Change **let** to **letting**
- ⬭ Change **her** to **she**
- ⬭ Change **sometime** to **sometimes**

3 Look at sentence 7 again.

> (7) Meows' favorite toy is a feather on a stick.

How should this sentence be changed?

- ⬭ Change **Meows'** to **Meow's**
- ⬭ Change **is** to **are**
- ⬭ Change **on** to **to**

GO ON

4 Look at sentence 9 again.

> (9) She also has a little toy mose on a string.

How should this sentence be changed?

- ⃝ Change *on* to **own**
- ⃝ Change *toy* to **toi**
- ⃝ Change *mose* to **mouse**

5 Look at sentence 10 again.

> (10) I move it around, and Meow watches it quiet.

How should this sentence be changed?

- ⃝ Change *I* to **Mine**
- ⃝ Change *watches* to **watchs**
- ⃝ Change *quiet* to **quietly**

GO ON

Read each introduction and the passage that follows it. Then read each question. Decide which is the best answer to each question. Mark the space for the answer you have chosen.

Marcus has written a report about an animal he saw at the zoo. Read it and think about what changes Marcus should make. Then answer the questions that follow.

A Lumpy, Bumpy Animal

(1) It looks like a pig with a bumpy face. (2) What is it? (3) It's a warthog!

(4) A baby warthog is very cute. (5) When it grows up, it gets bumps on its face and long hair on its back. (6) It isn't cute anymore! (7) It grows long, sharp tusks that help it fight off other animals. (8) It can run quickness on its long, thin legs.

(9) When it is hungry, itl'l eat berries and grass. (10) It gets doun on its knees. (11) Then it uses its snout to dig up roots and bugs.

(12) Female warthogs live together in a big group. (13) They help each other take care for the babies. (14) Each warthog mother knows hers babies are safe with the group.

GO ON

6 Look at sentence 8 again.

(8) It can run quickness on its long, thin legs.

How should this sentence be changed?

⬭ Change **can** to **could**

⬭ Change **run** to **running**

⬭ Change **quickness** to **quickly**

7 Look at sentence 9 again.

(9) When it is hungry, itl'l eat berries and grass.

How should this sentence be changed?

⬭ Change **When** to **Why**

⬭ Change **itl'l** to **it'll**

⬭ Change **and** to a comma (**,**)

8 Look at sentence 10 again.

(10) It gets doun on its knees.

How should this sentence be changed?

⬭ Change **doun** to **down**

⬭ Change **its** to **it's**

⬭ Change **knees** to **news**

GO ON ➡

9 Look at sentence 13 again.

> (13) They help each other take care for the babies.

How should this sentence be changed?

- ⬭ Change *They* to **Their**
- ⬭ Change *take* to **takes**
- ⬭ Change *for* to **of**

10 Look at sentence 14 again.

> (14) Each warthog mother knows hers babies are safe with the group.

How should this sentence be changed?

- ⬭ Change *Each* to **All**
- ⬭ Change *hers* to **her**
- ⬭ Change *with* to **out**

(STOP)

Writing: Written Composition

> Write an essay that tells why you like your favorite game.

Use a separate sheet of paper to plan your composition. Then write your composition on the lined pages that follow.

The tips in the box below will help you as you write.

REMEMBER—YOU SHOULD

❏ write about a game you like

❏ use opinion words and phrases to show your opinions

❏ give reasons and details so that the reader understands why you like the game

❏ use complete sentences

❏ try to use correct spelling, capitalization, punctuation, and grammar

_____

_____

_____

_____

_____

_____

_____

_____

_____

_____

_____

_____

_____

_____

_____

_____

_____

_____

_____

_____

_____

_____

_____

_____

_____